MEN RAISED BY WOMEN

What He Won't Tell Mom

By
John P. Dennis

Men Raised By Women
By John P. Dennis

ISBN 978-0-578-16299-7

John P. Dennis

CONTENTS

John P. Dennis

Acknowledgments

There are so many people who have contributed to the creation of this book. I am extremely fortunate to have so many loving family members and great friends who helped bring out my very first book.

To my loving wife Roshonda Nicole Dennis, you are my best friend, partner and confidant. Thank you for believing in me. Your patience and unflappable encouragement gave me the boost I needed when I doubted. I deeply appreciate you because you were the catalyst for many of the deep changes in my life. You are my partner for life.

To my mother and father, Flossie and John, for being the parents I needed. Your love and support throughout my life has made me into the man that I am today.

To my brothers and sisters: Thaddeus, Simone, Darnell and Adrianne ... you guys gave me the greatest family memories anyone could ask for. Thaddeus you were a great example of what a big brother should be! Simone you were an ear during my troubles and a leaning post when life was hard to figure out. Darnell you are the humblest and kindest soul I've ever known. You were my opportunity to be a big brother and I hope I lived up to your expectations. Adrianne I'm so proud of the beautiful young lady that you have become.

To my own sons John Jr, Daniel & Joseph, and my adopted daughter Katherine, I could write an entire book on the things you've taught me. Being a Dad has been the most wonderful experience of my life. You are the source of my motivation for writing this book.

My mentors are so numerous. I owe all of you such a debt of gratitude. I will try to go in order by my age as I grew older instead of weighing the impact you all made because you never know the full input of a mentor. To Mr. Hill, my 6th grade math teacher, my uncle Jake Johnson, Larry Buffer (USAF retired), Eric Washington (USAF retired), Jeff Holmes (USAF retired), Eric Lindquist (USAF), Chris Mitchell (USAF), Stephen Doersom (USAF retired), Jeff Mitchell (USAF), Pastor Ancil Carruthers, Pastor Dee Wayne Jones, Pastor Dick Chapman, Rick Wallace, Doug Burpee, William Brannon, Brian Nelson and Mr. Otto Williams. I pray I have not left someone out, as there were so many who have graciously guided my life.

Then there are those friends who made such an impact because they were walking with me. Their presence alone made a difference that cannot be tallied in life's vast equation. Cori Dennis, Walter Barrow, Marcelles Prather, Eric Pope, Thomas Webb, Russell King, Jessie Basaldua, Mark Eicholz, Matthew Mendenhall, Tim Lansdowne, Richard Scafe and James Clouse. I have a lot of friends but if you ever did me wrong...these are the people who would avenge me... (just kidding). But I wouldn't test it... there are truly too many to name. Thank you all.

I would be remiss if I discounted the numerous voices and input from distinguished individuals who helped me take this from a backyard conversation to an intelligent discussion that warrants attention. I am so blessed by your contributions. Thaddeus Dennis, Pastor Calvin Moore, Jamal Ferrari, Rodney Edison, and Professor Jolene Swain - your candid input made this work much more authentic and down-to-earth.

Finally, I would like to thank Mr. Wayne L. Wilson for his dedicated research and tenacity, and for his unrelenting efforts in helping me pull together this book. I could not have done it without you.

John P. Dennis

Introduction

"The search after the great men is the dream of youth, and the most serious occupation of manhood."

Ralph Waldo Emerson

John's Story

My parents divorced when I was 6 years old and access to my Dad was mainly over the summers. My mother moved us to a different county and the distance was too far for visits with my father during the week, and I suppose it was impractical for weekend visits as well. But we shared the summers and I really looked forward to them. Most of my cousins and aunts, and my grandmother, lived near Dad so going to visit him also meant getting to see most of my kinfolk, which was a real treat for me.

I had always proudly acknowledged that my mother was my hero for raising 3 boys and a girl primarily by herself; but as the years went on I became keenly aware of a deficit within my persona that left me unsure of how to navigate certain aspects of life. I remember praying my parents would get back together and even wishing my uncle Jake had been my father. Even when my mother re-married for a short time, after a little inner wrestling, I took advantage of having a father figure around and tapped into my stepfather. I'm not sure exactly how their marriage broke down but through some odd turn of events I caught my stepdad in a place he should not have been. That hurt me, and it hurt watching mom suffer and it hurt watching another father walk out of the door.

My teen years were even tougher. Mom did factory work. Dad was only available during the summers and rarely called. And, like all healthy teen boys my hormones were raging.

Thank God for Uncle Jake!

We had a weekly Bible study that we all did at home and it gave me consistent access to him. Uncle Jake was a Navy veteran and, back then, a police officer with a commanding presence. I couldn't tell you his actual height because he was like a giant to me, so when he said, "I need God in every part of my life," that's all I needed to hear. Real men need God - got it! I copied everything I could from him. He spent a lot of time with my older brother and I'd sneak into the conversation every chance I got. Later on I asked why he didn't pour into me the way he did my older brother. He replied, "I knew you'd be alright."

Uncle Jake saw the anguish his nephews were going through, and although I covet that time it's a fair approach to work with the oldest child knowing I was also copying and learning from my older brother as well. Okay then...step 1...Find God! Thanks Uncle Jake.

And, boy, did I find Him.

I put all my energy and effort into my faith. I paid attention at church and bible study and I realized Uncle Jake was right. Yet like any teen boy my hormones were on fire! By the time I got a little hair on my chest I found out a few of the ladies thought I was cute, making it hard to walk the line. Along with all this I was quite the nerd and proud of it. However, out of all my nerdy friends from high school I'd wager that I was the coolest of them. Still, the only advice I got about dating came from Mom and the church. Let's see..."Keep that thang in your pants!" and "He who looketh upon a woman and lusteth in his heart hath sinned already."

Uhhh, I'm confused! Because looking and lusting is teenage boy stuff: from that hidden Playboy book under the mattress (sorry Mom) to the first porn tapes one of our buddies got hold of. A teen boy can spot any fine girl within 20 yards and though I was taught well I was absolutely no different in that respect. But I survived the teen years and avoided the common teen pregnancy scenario. Then I went into the military and things really kicked up a notch.

By the age of 18 I joined the United States Air Force, by 19 I graduated at the top of the Air Traffic Control (ATC) School and by age 20 I had already become a fully certified Air Traffic Controller. In the military I immediately noticed how insecure I was in dealing with life, but thankfully, that male-dominated culture quickly exposed me to a high degree of character development. Older Sergeants took me under their wings and taught me tricks of the trade.

ATC training is one of the hardest professions you can choose. I remember trainers laying down some pretty harsh treatment and it really ticked me off. One of the older guys took me aside and told me in very direct terms... "Pick your battles youngster." He could tell I was about to stop biting my tongue and get a little retribution. Mom had said not to let anyone punk you out, but now I heard a way to deal with conflict that came from a highly respected man. It was completely different and everything resonating inside me felt right.

Soon it became the norm for me to attach to mentors on the job and at church. They became pseudo-father figures from whom I hung onto every word and watched every interaction to glean nuggets of wisdom. I noticed other younger men doing exactly the same thing with me; so as I was being fathered, mentored and grounded, I was doing the same for others that were further downstream than I was. There were other guys clinging to the same boat I was in.

I worked the partying out of my system by age 21 in Tokyo, Japan and became active in my local church. In addition, I often volunteered as a Big Brother and mentor at the local work release center. In fact, if my daughter brought home a young man with my credentials, now he'd get the nod of approval. Yet, in retrospect, on the inside I realized I had not fully developed into manhood.

My poor ex-wife bore the brunt of those developmental years. Looking back I can honestly say it was the underlying hinge of many of our fights. I married by the age of 23 and although I was financially stable, moral, and responsible, it is fair to say that I was a young 23 and too young for marriage. And if I wasn't too young then it's certainly safe to say I was developmentally immature. I always joked that I was a late bloomer and though I prefer it that way, I must admit I was internally lacking essential things. They were things my mother could not see and never could have helped me with.

Marriage brought all those issues to the surface at the same time. I recall an instance when one of our cars needed an oil change. My wife asked me if I was going to do it, but not knowing how to change the oil I covered up my embarrassment and insecurity by constantly declaring, "I'm an Air Traffic Controller." So I took the car to a garage and paid for the oil change. There is nothing wrong with paying for an oil change but that wasn't really the issue.

I began facing a host of life issues that I felt ill prepared for. It seemed like it made me less of a man and I felt even sillier when I paid to have things done, and watched guys do something as simple as unclog a pipe in front of me. Those challenges, however, were easier to overcome than the emotional weights. I learned how to do the majority of the "handyman" stuff. The worst issue is that I had become one of the leaning posts and counselors for my own mother. It was a terrible burden as I consoled my mother through her divorce, financial struggles and life choices. That weighed negatively on my own marriage and put a further strain on my relationship with my wife. How could she ask me to stop being there for my mother?

John P. Dennis

What is the right balance?

What do you do when your mother calls you bawling her eyes out at 4 AM?

These are difficult questions for an MRW who has watched his mother suffer and sacrifice over the years, and has tried to be there for his mom when she needed help. You know her problems all too well and you're haunted by the idea that you are doing so well and she is struggling.

It took years of sorting through the situations, books and mentors, as well as a life coach to really see the unhealthy fallout from that kind of parental bond. There were lots of issues and while I was working on them I was mentoring young men at work and at church, raising my own sons, and trying to navigate married life. After nearly 15 years of marriage we divorced, and although this is not a book about marriage it can help in some areas of marriage where the subjects apply.

I pray it does.

Now my greatest fear was upon me...my own 3 boys had now suffered through my greatest pain...divorce. Once we were officially divorced, our three sons were at the ages of 15, 13, and 11. Their mom received full custody due to my work assignments overseas in Afghanistan. The repercussions of the divorce were not only devastating; I was also haunted by the guilt that ravaged me for not being around my boys. I had always been an active dad...attending every game, sporting event, and occasionally even coaching. I loved being involved in their school events, and engaged in their social affairs. It was a troubling time for me and I was bedeviled by all the things I needed to sort out, the most important being that my boys were not adversely affected by our separation and divorce, and that they were grounded and secure as they took those sometimes uncertain steps into life.

Furthermore, it was difficult because this was the most critical juncture of their lives. This was a time of adolescence and puberty; a time for me to be in their lives to answer those questions. Unfortunately, due to the circumstances of my work, I began to feel like I had been exiled at the most important time of their lives – a time when they needed Dad to help them navigate their path to manhood and deal with the sheer physicality (puberty and testosterone) and emotions of learning how to be a good man. It hurt because I initially felt like I was relegated to the role of only being a part-time father.

Notwithstanding, I did, and do, as much as I can despite the situation. Thank goodness for modern society's technology! We spoke by email and phone, but if you know teenage boys...unless you're a cute girl they really don't want to be on the phone all that much. At times we'd Skype or FaceTime, and conversations slipped into bland replays:

"How are you?"

"Fine."

"How have things been going?"

"Good."

We weren't solving world problems and they weren't the most stimulating conversations of all time, so it took a lot of work to extract what was going on with them until I started using playbacks from my teen years. I'd basically start out with something such as, "Wow, when I was 14, I was always walking around with an uncomfortable hard-on...that stuff happens to guys...does that embarrass you like it did me?" Then, Bam!!! The conversation would take off because I moved from just being Dad to someone that went through the same challenges they were experiencing. That's how I got them to talk and thus far it's worked pretty well over the years.

Logistics, such as living in different states, can be a problem but my relationship with my sons is vitally essential even though I live in Georgia and they live in California. Thankfully I can afford to fly them over for a portion of the summer and Christmas each year, and most recently for my

John P. Dennis

wedding. But primarily we spend time by phone & Facebook prompts, plus photos. My sons are now well into their teens and my oldest is nineteen. You can make a case that a lot of their personality and character had set in by the time I was divorced, but I'd say that's also when they started to wrestle with major surges of testosterone, girl questions, career choices, questions about God and life's realities. When a boy is older he has more mature thinking and better analytical abilities so he is able to ask more in-depth questions about things. For instance, he may have accepted that babies come from mom's belly when he was 5, but when he is 10, he will ask how the baby got into mom's belly. And, they are able to see your faults as adults so it's time to help them take in life more maturely.

I know how they need me because I know what I required as a youth. My ex-wife and I are able to work together and co-parent on things and for that I'm truly grateful. I try to stay plugged in, to be there for them, and ultimately to be an influence for good in their lives. A few instances have come up that remind me of situations growing up and I spotted them quickly. My boys need me more than ever before.

A few years passed and I married again to a wonderful young lady. She had a young son and teen daughter already and we'd get into real debates about how some things should be done with the kids. We talked it out a lot and she really began to see that all I was doing was providing male perspective and input. Things as small as making the toddler sleep in his room were real emotional challenges for both of them. We ended up deeply delving into the issues surrounding the way moms might keep the chicks in the nest too long or let emotions leverage too much in child-rearing decisions. She had never really gotten feedback from a male perspective before and had to make the best decisions she could, coming from a matriarchal household herself. It gave me insight on how my own mother had arrived at some of the approaches she took while rearing us. As we began piecing it all together we kept seeing MRW issues everywhere.

My wife strongly encouraged me to write a book about it and convinced me it was sorely needed. She'd quiz me endlessly over behavior she encountered from men she dealt with over the years. Inevitably it kept leading back to the same assessment. They had been raised by women, and more on point, lacked masculine perspectives and development in some areas, as I had also. That is not to say they possessed feminine tendencies but instead were caught up in situations where the umbilical cord was still attached to mom and they tended to be more emotional than rational.

We started using the term MRWs jokingly, but it began to take on a real presence and I think the most persuasive comments came when I'd hear my stepdaughter begin to use the term to refer to some of the guys who tried to date her. I told my sons about my intent to write this book and to my astonishment they were fully engaged and truly believed it needed to be talked about.

That's when I got serious.

My boys keep me constantly attuned to the internal challenges young males are coping with, and if "character determines destiny" then the most "on-target" approach would be to put some real emphasis on their character development and stability. If I required help, and they needed help, then surely others do as well.

Was this one of the elephants in the room rarely addressed?

As I discussed the notion of writing a book with close friends I was met with overwhelming support and encouragement. Just upon seeing the title and a draft of the chapter headings some of my friends have already vowed to purchase multiple copies proclaiming, "I know exactly who to give this to!" It appeared everyone seemed to have a connective story that underscored the subjects I wanted to discuss. I even bounced it off a few strangers in passing just to get a reaction and each time people wanted to hear these concepts fleshed out and have the discussion.

Before I proceed forward, it is important to note that MRWs can have successful careers and noteworthy achievements. I amassed a laundry list of successes myself along the way. It's not a negative statement to be identified as an MRW, yet I want to touch upon those invisible and intangible parts that give MRWs hidden struggles in their manhood and relationships.

I began intently reading and researching any available information, news, and media reports about the tremendous rise of single mothers and fatherless homes. I was taken aback by how many of these sources and publications cited negative statistics. A crisis exists that cannot be ignored, simply due to an increase in the absence of fathers participating in their sons' upbringing – regardless of the multitude of reasons.

My primary objectives in this manuscript are to act as an advocate for boys making a healthy transition to manhood; to offer pertinent information, guidance, and a male perspective to single moms; to make an appeal to fathers who have been on the periphery to be more responsible and actively involved with their sons; and finally, to encourage those caring men in our society, who see a mother struggling to raise her sons, to step forward and contribute in whatever ways possible to help raise her boys to be healthy, responsible, and contributing adults that benefit our world.

I shed the observer skin, because my sons, like me, were dealing with the trauma of their parents' separation and impending divorce. Plus their mother, due to the living arrangement, would now become the consistent physical presence in their daily lives. Would they be able to develop their faith in God? Would they feel it was their fault we got divorced? Would they think that Dad abandoned them? Would they attach to some other man? Would they make good choices on women, careers and life issues?

The divorce coupled with my experiences growing up was the final impetus that drove me to enlighten myself and find out everything I could about the single mother scenario and its effects on the children – specifically in this case – raising boys. And this process generated a variety of questions such as: What is the impact of a father? What happens when boys on the playground have never had a dad in the home? Do they overcompensate by being more aggressive? Less? Do MRWs all think the same way about family, marriage, child-rearing, and life?

I recall in my neighborhood during my early teen years in the 80's that only a few kids in class were in single parent homes. None of the friends in my circle had teenage mothers or lived with grandparents, though I knew of a few that did. It was not the norm. And sadly, there were stigmas, stereotypes, and unnecessary pressures attached to being an unmarried mother. I assumed there was obviously some effect but what was it? And, is there something that can be done to help those individuals work on a healthy development track towards manhood?

I began to pay close attention to all the media reports and dialogue on single parenthood, and took copious notes on the impact that fatherless homes has on children. I suspected some kids raised without a father might be burdened with problems, but I had no idea to what degree society was impacted by homes without a paternal figure.

The statistics were frightening!

It was alarming to read the plethora of new studies released pronouncing the negative effect on children of fatherless homes. It was even more shocking to read in the report released by the U.S. Census Bureau that single mothers raise one in four children. Approximately 82% of custodial parents are mothers. In the African American community, 72% of black children are brought up in households without a father.

We will go into the myriad of reasons for these distressing statistics in a later chapter, but for now it is important to note that there are millions of children who do not live with their dads. The deprivation of male attention can't be good no matter how you want to analyze it. And it breaks my heart to know there are millions of kids crying out for a missing dad they needed yesterday!

I've watched the pundits and politicians storming the talk shows armed with their books and statistics about how critical it is to have a dad in the home to ensure the healthy development of a child. But it's not always possible and can't be helped in numerous cases. Some of those dads needed to be kicked out of the house or prevented from boarding with their negativity and bad influence.

I've watched feminists who, on the other hand, argue with their own statistics that single mothers raising sons can be a good thing and that it is more accepted by society. They claim that boys raised by women often tend to be more sensitive and caring, and know how to treat women properly. But, these same feminists have difficulty addressing the financial (and grim) statistics regarding the adverse consequences many of these children encounter.

We may choose to try and ignore it, but there are facts and figures substantiated by decades of research that are truly irrefutable: children raised by single parents overall do not fare as well as those reared in a traditional two-parent household. According to the U.S. Census Bureau it is estimated that six in ten children raised in single-mother households are at or below the poverty line. Children in single-mother homes are more likely to abuse drugs, have measurably lower academic achievement, lower self-esteem, more emotional problems, a greater risk of incarceration, and more.

I've had the opportunity to read many books about single parenting, including some very good ones I recommend that you'll see in the section on "Further Reading". Many of the books I found on single parenting were written by women who are single mothers, including those who have raised sons, who discuss the obstacles and positives of child rearing alone. But there were a lack of books offering a male perspective from the standpoint of having been brought up by a single mother. Though I've tried hard to maintain my objectivity there is a need for a paternal voice in helping single mothers address the issues of raising a son in a society fraught with obstacles specific to our young men.

First of all, I want to make it clear – I am not an academician, a scholar, a marriage & family therapist, a psychologist, or a specialist in the area of parental studies. I'm a concerned Dad, who delved into the area of single mothers raising sons. I am writing this book from a male perspective as a guide to help single mothers understand how males think and what things occur to us growing up. I have intellectual facts and statistics to offer, but this book is primarily "straight talk" and another voice for moms to contemplate while bringing up their male child.

Despite the negativity you may have heard and encountered out there, no one is pointing the finger here. This is not a "Let's Blame Mom" book. I am hardly interested in blaming you...my main objective is to EMPOWER you! This is not written to call you a bad Mom or even to call Dad a bad father. Dads can just as easily be blamed, but that doesn't provide a solution either. I understand and empathize with how difficult it is for a single mother to raise a child, especially if you're struggling with finances and working multiple jobs. You don't need any more criticism – you need help! This book should be used as a guide and another voice to assist you in raising an emotionally and physically healthy male who will contribute to and positively impact our world.

There is no perfect model, of course, and even in a two-parent home there exists a host of problems; however, this effort is to acknowledge the issues that arise when the father is not available. I'm aware of how all you moms out there are doing what you can to make things work. I applaud and praise you for your noteworthy efforts, and commend all of you who have already successfully raised wonderful kids!

One of the issues I'm focusing on in this guide is what might be called the "Side Effects." For example, you might take an allergy medicine to stop itching and discover that the medication's side effects leave you feeling drowsy or groggy. In the same way, moms forced to adjust for the lack of a dad in the home may find that the side effects have a pronounced bearing on the family. Those particular side effects are one of the things I plan to discuss with you in this book.

Another important goal of mine is that this book serves as a tool for moms to structure some of their dealings with their male children, and perhaps even the fathers, in a beneficial manner. You will read personal accounts and heartfelt admissions from other men in this book about their experiences growing up with a single mother, and I hope it will proffer examples to you that will provide some relevancy to you as you raise your son.

Ultimately what you gain from the information, opinions, personal observations, experiences, and advice is up to you. My incentive is to offer a self-help guide primarily to single mothers bringing up male children. I would love for Dad, if he is available, to read this and be inspired to make a sincere effort to become a co-parent if he hasn't already. And lastly, I hope a single mom will not be too closed off to leave the door open for a good male figure (can be a relative, friend, coach, etc.) who wants to be involved, to enter, and prove to be a great role model for her child.

Just remember, I've got your back and we are in this together – so let's get to it.

John P. Dennis

Chapter One

The Modern Family

Hi Mom!

There it is...

I could be sitting on the couch in the living room reading a newspaper with the TV broadcasting a sports program and I'll hear that enthusiastic greeting shouted by an athlete during an interview or waving and posing for the television camera after a spectacular play in a sporting event. Or it might be an emotional outburst from a performer thanking both God and mother for their talents and being there for them during the highs and lows; or from a person on the street mugging for the camera. And you know what? I don't even blink when I hear it. I'm so used to it. It's a subliminal thing...as common as a period following a sentence.

Of course, I'm exaggerating, but I think we can all agree, "Hi Mom" is the most frequent phrase you'll hear from a person on TV, even when the dad lives at home. Now understand, I'm not angry about it. This is not soapbox material and I'm not complaining. I sincerely view mothers as the supreme nurturers of the universe and they deserve to take a primary position at the head of any "media" table. Success stories abound from men raised by single mothers. It's well documented that President Barack Obama was raised by a single mother and his grandparents. In fact, two of the last three presidents were raised by single mothers during part of their childhood, proving that kids can grow up to be successful.

If you ask the people in the social expression industry where moms' and dads' positions are in the social hierarchy of greeting cards and related gift items, without question Mother's day is one of the largest consumer holidays, not far behind Christmas and Valentine's Day.

Father's Day ranks slightly above Groundhog Day in terms of popularity...

Historically speaking, society has not been particularly kind to single moms. Mothers have been subjected to all types of stigmas, stereotypes, and unnecessary pressures. Mothers have been blamed for the evils of the world. Even with the father being a part of the household, women were held accountable for everything that occurred while rearing their sons, including whether they grew up to be bad or good. Mothers were blamed for children contracting an illness they never caused. Single mothers today are still automatically stamped with the label of being welfare cases and financially unstable. It is instantly assumed that their lives are filled with struggle and chaos.

A woman who chose to have a child out of wedlock was frequently eyed with suspicion. Her life was viewed as terrible compared to the "happy" life of a married woman. Many women complain that remains the case. The press is still guilty of attaching a mark of disgrace, a "Scarlet Letter", to how women are perceived as single mothers. Many single mothers complain that oftentimes mass media makes them feel as if they should be ashamed for being unmarried and raising a child. They are condemned for selfishly choosing to bring a child into the world without the presence of a father, and are in essence faulted for bringing down the institution of family.

Naysayers fail to realize that many of the women bringing up a child alone started out in committed relationships and never expected or aspired to be a single parent. The media has hoisted the derogatory term "Baby Momma" on them for begetting illegitimate children and not being involved with the father. The stereotype is that all single mothers are unemployed and receiving government assistance.

Thankfully it's gotten somewhat better and the stigma affixed to single mothers is not as all-encompassing as it once was. Single parenting is establishing itself as the norm. Over the years, following the incredibly rapid growth of single parenthood, society has begrudgingly accepted its pronounced impact on the American family's structure. Many conservative critics are panicking and bemoaning the erosion of the nuclear family, which is coupled with the fear that its cancerous effect is ultimately leading to the disintegration of the American family and therefore a healthy society.

As commonly reported, one in two marriages in America end in divorce and in the majority of the cases mothers are awarded sole or primary residential custody of the children. Jane Juffer in her book, *Single Mother: The Emergence of the Domestic Intellectual* states:

"The Emergence of the Domestic Intellectual elaborates on the consequences of this decision: What is produced is a family structure that both diverges from and relies on the nuclear family, as mothers are awarded custody precisely because they have always been the primary caregivers. Mothers also bear the burden, then, of the conservative backlash against the breakdown of the nuclear family norm, for it becomes our responsibility to prove that divorce will not harm our children and indeed, the nation."

Critics wonder what happened to the generations of families headed by the likes of Ozzie and Harriet Nelson, Lucy and Ricky Ricardo, Rob and Laura Petrie, Ward and June Cleaver, John and Olivia Walton, Cliff and Clair Huxtable, Tom and Joan Bradford and those eight kids, Mike and Carol Brady, George and Louise Jefferson, Charles and Caroline Ingalls, Coach Eric and Tami Taylor, Steven and Elyse Keaton, Fred and Wilma Flintstone, and so forth.

Nothing happened. They're still on TV where you left them. You can still watch these family-oriented shows pretty much any time you want. And despite the sometimes dysfunctional lives of the actors off the set, people wax nostalgic and long for their families to be just like the idealized ones they watch on television.

The nuclear family with the father as the conventional breadwinner and decision maker, and the stay-at-home mom with at least two kids, represented for many folks the perfect ideal of what a family should be. However, the reality is there has never been any one type of family. United States history has shown that families have been torn apart and reassembled – slavery and the barbarism of selling off family members being the most extreme and blatant example.

According to Dr. Peggy Drexler in her book *Raising Boys Without Men* it wasn't until around the 1920s that the majority of children lived in homes with the father as the breadwinner and the wife as the homemaker. The kids went to school instead of working for wages. She debates the proposition by many scholars that the largest increase in unwed motherhood was during the sexual revolution of the 1960s. Drexler claims that there was a far more significant increase during the Great Depression, which even tripled between 1940 and 1958 with husbands abandoning their wives and children, and that out-of-wedlock sex soared during World War II.

In modern times children are raised by single men and women, grandparents, adoptive parents, cohabitating unmarried parents, gay men and lesbian parents, and stepparents. Critics need not be alarmed; nuclear families remain represented on TV today just like in real life.

On another note there are a multitude of popular reality-based shows (i.e. *Maury*) based on individuals taking paternity tests to determine whether they are the father of a child. Viewers are glued to their TV sets as Maury announces: "You ARE the Father" or "You are NOT the Father!" And it's not unusual to see a mother who is right about the father of her child, or a relieved man who has been wrongly accused of being a father, spontaneously break out into an outrageously happy dance. No matter

John P. Dennis

how embarrassed many of us may feel about these antics, it's apparent a large number of the children on the show were birthed out of wedlock; an indication, good and bad, of the imprint that single parenthood has made, and that society has recognized there are a proliferation of kids being raised by mostly single mothers. Many of these women have never been married and a large number bore kids with more than one man.

Choice and the tremendous increase in divorce have much to do with the marked rise of single mother households. Overall, single-parent families have tripled in the United States since 1960 and much of this can be attributed to women exercising their independence. Studies have shown during the past four decades that the number of single moms has skyrocketed from 3.5 million in 1970 to currently 10 million.

Women are offered more options now. They no longer feel handcuffed to a marriage because of society's religious and social pressures. Actually, many unwed women justify their decision to keep their child because of their Christian faith and opposition to abortion. In an article entitled "The New Math of the Single Mother: Why the ranks of America's unmarried moms keep growing" the authors, June Carbone and Naomi Cahn, state that compared to a decade ago the rate of American women getting pregnant unintentionally is significantly higher, and that the United States has one of the highest unintended birth rates in the developed world.

Unlike their parents and grandparents, women don't fear being shadowed by social stigma until their kids are grown up. In today's climate they don't have to stay in marriages with abusive or philandering husbands – they can just leave accompanied by the support of family, friends, and support groups. Young unwed mothers are not hidden from sight or shipped off somewhere to have their babies in secret and then put them up for adoption.

Decades ago women didn't have the job opportunities that are currently available to support themselves and their children. Even if they can barely sustain the family women will choose to be alone over an unhappy marriage. Also, women who are doing well economically are not waiting for the "perfect" man to enter their lives...they have grown tired of waiting and decide to have a child figuring they will deal with whatever consequences come their way.

Something else that should be mentioned and that plays a significant role in the increase of single mothers is that the U.S. economy reflects their limited choices. Carbone and Cahn explain:

"Between 1979 and 2007, every group of men except for college graduates saw its income fall, while every group of women except for high school dropouts enjoyed an increase in income, according to the Pew Research Center. This means that there are more men at the top and bottom of the income ladder, and a larger group of women in the middle with fewer acceptable partners. Moreover, the men at the bottom have lost ground not only in terms of income, but in rising rates of unemployment, job instability, lack of community involvement and a corresponding loss of status. In these circumstances, marrying and staying married can be more burden than boon. As one divorced mother we interviewed told us, 'I can take care of myself and the kid. I just can't take care of myself, the kid and him.'"

The bottom line is that one of the major reasons for higher divorce rates is that a lot of women won't stay with men who are making less money than they are. And this can be a conundrum because the problem with the men is that due to the economic inequality in our system they often become troubled because of the loss of status, and depressed from losing their jobs, accepting lower pay, or dealing with chronic unemployment. Men who are fired or laid-off are less likely to help around the home and may end up drinking or indulging in substance abuse, or abusing their wives or intimate partners, leading to arrests and imprisonment.

Melissa Ludtke, in her book *On Our Own: Unmarried Motherhood in America*, writes: "When young fathers can't do what they believe a good father should do – provide financially for his family – their relationships with children and girlfriends often unravel. As one mother said to me, 'Welfare becomes the man.'"

John P. Dennis

Coinciding with this line of thinking, women determine to get divorced or, if they are single, pass on marrying the father of their child because he's more trouble than he's worth.

Once considered the bastion of poor women and minorities, the growing trend of having children outside of marriage has become the norm for single motherhood. Of interest are the following single-mother statistics I have gathered from primarily the U.S. Census Bureau report:

- *Single mothers make up the majority of single-parent families. Out of 12 million single-parent families in 2014, more than 80% were headed by single mothers; 83% have children under 18 years of age.*

- *Approximately 4 out of 10 children were born to unwed mothers. Two-thirds of those children were born to mothers under the age of 30.*

- *One in four children under the age of 18 (17.4 million) are being raised without a father and nearly half live below the poverty line.*

- *Demographics: 49% of single mothers never married; 51% are divorced, separated, or widowed. Of this number, two-thirds are White, one-third African American, and one-quarter Hispanic. One-third have college degrees; one-sixth have not completed high school.*

- *According to Census data, poverty is not the norm for single mothers (as some would like to believe). Still, single mothers are more likely be poorer than married couples. In 2013 the poverty rate for single mothers was 39.6%, compared to 7.6% for married couple families. In addition, more than half (51.9%) of single mothers do live in extreme poverty with incomes below half of the federal poverty level. Poverty rates by ethnicity are*

– *Native American (52.8%), African American (46.3%), Hispanic (46.5%), White (31.6%), and Asian (24.0%).*

- *Approximately one-third of unintended pregnancies are to unmarried women in their 20s.*

- *African American and Hispanic women have the highest teen pregnancy rates at 100 and 84 respectively per 1,000 women aged 15-19; Whites have the lowest with 38 pregnancies per 1,000.*

- *Of the 1.6 million children born out of wedlock in the United States in 2013, 15% were born to teenagers under age 20; 37% were born to women ages 20-24.*

- *African American women tend to have more children outside of marriage than any other racial or ethnic group; 72% of births to African American women were non-marital births.*

- *The children most likely to grow up in single-parent households are the ones born to young unmarried mothers. Census data estimates that more than two-thirds of these mothers end up on welfare.*

- *Single mothers in the United States have higher poverty rates than single mothers in other high-income countries. This is accounted for by the fact that many employed single mothers are earning poverty wages; 40% of U.S. single parents were employed in low-wage jobs, which is exceedingly high compared to single parents in peer countries.*

The preceding information reveals the disturbing and unvarnished facts from the most recent Census data. Compared to married households there is a higher risk for children in single-mother homes to abuse drugs, produce lower academic achievement scores, have low self-esteem, suffer from more emotional problems, act up in class and/or drop out, and face a greater risk of imprisonment, teenage pregnancies (babies making babies),

John P. Dennis

and so forth. In addition, seven in ten African American children are raised in homes without a father. One of the significant reasons for this is the disproportionate number of African American men that are incarcerated.

Attorney Lisa Bloom, who raised her kids as a single mother, discusses in her book, *SWAGGER: 10 Urgent Rules for Raising Boys in an Era of Failing Schools, Mass Joblessness, and Thug Culture*, how it seems like fathers in divorced and never-married families have practically vanished. Bloom reports:

"One in five fathers who live apart from their children say they visit with them more than once a week, and an additional 29 percent see their children at least once a month. But for 21 percent of these fathers, the visits take place just a few times per year. And for 27 percent there are no visits at all. If you add together those last two categories that means that almost half the kids in single-mom households have no real dad to speak of in their lives. In another study nearly one-third of fathers who do not live with their children say they talk or exchange e-mails with them less than once a month. Occasional e-mails? Is that what fatherhood has been reduced to?"

Some of you may find these grim statistics interesting and want to know more; others of you may be completely turned off and feeling like, "I don't need to read any more of this stuff – leave me alone!"

I can't because I want to help.

I understand that rearing a child alone is hard for anyone, especially if you're financially strapped and struggling with poverty. I realize that single moms can at times be overstressed and overwhelmed. To reiterate, I'm writing this book as a guide to help mothers in their efforts to raise their sons and to encourage fathers to play a greater role in their sons' upbringing, and to recruit caring men to be role models and to take boys under their wings.

My end goal in this book is to promote the development of young men.

Hopefully, you'll stay with me and continue reading with the understanding that these stats I've presented are not meant to chastise you, or depress you, or inhibit you from raising your child. The statistics in this book are meant to inform you, not undermine you. They are to help you move forward with an increased awareness and knowledge of the risks you may encounter so you can utilize this information to prove wrong those overly analytical soothsayers out there who predict you won't be able to raise your son properly.

I felt it was important to explore the history of and reasons why there has been such an increase in the trend toward single parenthood. My foremost concern, despite what you see statistically, is not whether you are rich, poor, middle class or whatever...no two single mothers are the same, nor are they a part of some monolithic group, as some so-called scholars want you to believe. I want to assist mothers in understanding what males need and to help boys learn how to be accountable for their actions.

In the chapters to follow you will learn more about the 11 character strengths I think are vital to incorporate into the development of boys in their transition to manhood: Self Respect, Respect for Others, Respect for Authority, Respect for Property, Self-Discipline, Integrity, Responsibility, Trustworthiness, Fairness, Caring, and Citizenship.

At all economic levels a son faces many of the same risks I outlined to you. Being affluent may decrease some of the risks, but it doesn't guarantee you'll raise an outstanding young man. Boys need positive male influences in their lives in order to one day be healthy and contributing adults. I want to see boys grow up to become outstanding individuals in our society. I'm sure you feel the same way. I hope by writing this book I can, through you, contribute to that process.

John P. Dennis

Chapter Two

I Don't Need A Man! Okay, That's Fine...But What About Your Son?

"The young boy cannot grow up to be a male without models to demonstrate the tremendous generosity, the spirit, the willingness to sacrifice for the community that the word male implies in the positive sense."

Robert Bly (author, poet)

When I first delved into writing this book I decided to share the concept with various women to get a feel for what they thought about the material. Most were very positive and excited about the promise of, and the need for, a book of this nature. Yet, what also erupted were emotional and defensive reactions from a few women regarding the subject. It was as if the very act of my writing an MRW book questioned the capability of a woman to raise a son without a father.

"I don't need a man in my life to help me raise my son!"

This chorus I've heard repeatedly from single moms whenever the subject is broached. The operative words here are **my life**. And my retort is, "But what about your son's life?"

One thing we need to understand is that although there may be a tremendous rise in single parent families, single mothers have raised boys without a man in the house for thousands of years. But it is also important to note that many women who achieved success in their sons' upbringing stress that they found great male role models ranging from uncles and grandfathers to friends, sports coaches, teachers, clergymen, and so on.

On another occasion I talked to a woman who adamantly contended that women could raise boys without a father or pivotal male's influence. Finally, I asked her pointblank, "Did you tell your son about childbirth?" She replied, of course she did, and talked about how she taught him the proper way to treat women, etc.

"No," I said, "Did you tell him that even though his wife's vagina is stretched out to unbelievable dimensions during childbirth it will revert back to the same cuddly spot that he was accustomed to?"

She got real quiet after that...and although I knew I was being very graphic, I think she realized my point – that male input, "guy talk" is vitally important to a young man. Intimate issues like this, and going through puberty, a young man finds difficult to discuss with his mother even though she may feel or think she's in a place where she can talk to him about everything.

In *The Invisible Presence*, Michael Gurian relays a story about a man who shares with his men's group how humiliated he felt as a young man to have his mother accompany him on his visit to the doctor's office after suffering a football injury.

"The gash was on my thigh, right by my groin. I begged and begged my mother to let the doctor examine me without her there. She thought I was really silly. We went in there and I had to take my clothes off. I had a few pubic

hairs by then. In front of the doctor she clapped her hands. 'Oh, look, my little boy's becoming a man!' I was so embarrassed I couldn't speak. I think even the doctor was embarrassed. She never got it. She never understood I just didn't want her there."

There are issues that young males will never discuss with their mothers no matter how close their relationship is. Dr. Meg Meeker, M.D. wrote in her article "A Mother's Son":

"Mothers love to talk to their sons, but they shouldn't always expect much of a response. Women are comfortable discussing their intimate feelings; boys and men are not, and sometimes cannot. Their own feelings are a bottled up mystery even to themselves. But teenage boys in particular still want to know that their mother is interested in their feelings, even if they cannot articulate them. And while this can be comforting and necessary, at times it can drive boys crazy. Mothers must be sensitive towards their son's responses. For instance, since women tend to discuss their intimate thoughts and feelings with one another, mothers naturally transfer this behavior to relationships with their sons. If something is wrong, a mother asks what it is. Young boys usually don't know. And if they do, sometimes they will divulge what it is; sometimes they won't."

So when I hear a woman say, I don't need a man...my reply is - you may not, but your son does. You've expressed how you feel, but do you really know how your son feels about not having the presence of his father, stepfather, or strong and positive male role models in his life? And I'm not talking about when you ask him whether he wants to see his dad and he grunts, "No" or "I don't care", because he's aware of how angry you are at his father. He won't be honest and admit it hurts him and then have to listen to you give him flack about it.

Have you probed below the surface of his feelings? Sure, it's tough when you don't have a partner and you're the only one paying those bills while trying to keep your mind open and hear what your son is really saying. The communication may not be verbal. It may only be visible in his body language – he's pouting, or spending too much time alone or an excessive amount of time on his computer, or always hanging out with his boys.

Look, I totally understand and empathize when a single mother chooses to do whatever is necessary to raise her son alone; especially if you're dealing with financial hardship and the baby's living and breathing daddy is around the corner, refusing to step up to his responsibilities. I get that. All I'm saying is, in the meantime keep doing what's necessary to provide your son with as wonderful a life as you can possibly offer him.

Some of you may even think it's better to wait until the right person enters your love life and then you can incorporate him into your family. Wonderful, if it happens naturally...but, remember, it's not about putting your son's needs on hold until you find "Mr. Right" and then "voila" - all your problems are solved! Now you and your son have the perfect man filling the void in your lives! Uh, uh...your son can't wait on the perfect situation. And what if it doesn't work out and you're stuck confronting new issues if the man moves out?

In the *New York Times* article "Two Classes, Divided by 'I Do'" Jason DeParle tells a story about a woman who dated a man for a year and then let him move into her house with her two young daughters and son; mainly because he would help with the children and the bills. The boy adored him and exclaimed to her, "I'm not the only boy anymore; we're going to do boy stuff!"

"What's boy stuff?" his mother asked.

"We're going to play video games and shoot Nerf guns and play Legos," he said.

"We do that now," she said.

"Yeah, but you're not a boy."

You get the point. Nevertheless, the relationship turned into a disaster and the woman ended up calling the police to get the boyfriend out of her house. It was especially tough on her son who had developed an attachment to him.

Maybe it's easier to understand if we look at the opposite scenario. I haven't mentioned her up until now, but after my divorce my 12-year-old adopted daughter came to live with me for a couple of years. It was a challenge but I'm no slouch...I took her shopping, to the salon to get her hair done and even tried to do a few hairstyles myself. I had already been a parent for fourteen years so how different could this be? Almost immediately my mother and sister began pointing out things I was missing with her. I remember when my sister asked me if my daughter had started having a menstrual cycle. We all know it's part of the female development but when you're a man you just don't pick up on it. So when I got to Walmart to get her sanitary napkins I couldn't figure out if I was to get her pads or tampons? Can a girl who is a virgin even use a tampon? DAD DOESN'T KNOW! It's a riddle, and how was I gonna know whether she had a heavy or light flow? I don't even wanna know! And how do I explain the menstrual pains along with the emotional changes she would encounter? Thank God for the ladies in my family who stepped up!

Just as I could never intuitively know the nuances of female teen development issues, a mother does not know male teen development issues. We have blind spots in certain areas when it comes to the opposite gender, so don't feel bad about it, and realize it's not a critique, it's a reality. And this is just with physical development. There are just as many emotional and psychological changes going on with a male teen that are outside of a mother's experience and view.

Yes, in the early stages of development a son needs his mother to nurture him. Once he nears puberty, most scholars agree that it's time to insert male influences in his life. He's got a ton of questions spinning around in his head about the changes his body and mind are going through...even if he doesn't verbalize them – and chances are he won't. He may be confused about what's happening.

Another cliché I hear all the time from single mothers is, "I'm a mother and a father to my son..."

No you're not. You're his mother – period.

Don't get me wrong...I understand the source of this statement. You're doing double duty...you may be overstressed and working 2-3 jobs...you don't have a mate in your life to spell relief for you and give you some time to yourself to breathe. After hearing it enough times, your son may start to mimic you (even as an adult) by agreeing, my mother is my mother and father. And I sincerely applaud you for toughing it out and trying to raise a child on your own.

But you're NOT his father.

Clinical Professor Jolene Swain, a faculty member of the USC School of Social Work, is even more emphatic about it. She is a single mother with a son who wrote, directed, and produced the exceptional documentary film No Greater Bond, which provides an intimate look at the lives of Jolene and 3 other single mothers raising sons and the multiple challenges they face. She addressed this issue in a recent interview:

"I did the documentary to jumpstart things, to show that there should be educational workshops for women and single mothers and also a call out to men to be prepared to be there, to help us mentor and coach our sons in a positive way because that's what we need. If we're going to release them, we need a male community that's going to be there to receive them. Mothers need to be educated and it helps to come from another woman to tell her you can't teach your son how to become a man – because you're not a man! Black women are socialized to think of themselves as the man and a woman...mother and father – no you're not! It's not true! We have to stop thinking that way! We are not both! And sometimes I'm not very popular because I tell women that. And I am not going to stop saying it! That's been my struggle or challenge in getting parent education off the ground regarding this because African American women don't want to hear it. The attitude is I can do it alone!"

President Barack Obama is often cited as the greatest evidence in proving how single mothers can raise their child successfully without a man. Nonetheless, you must keep in mind that the President not only harshly criticized absentee fathers but has spoken frequently about how much he regrets that his father did not play a more significant role in his upbringing.

"I didn't have a dad in the house. And I was angry about it, even though I didn't necessarily realize it at the time...Too many fathers are AWOL, missing from too many lives and too many homes...I know the toll it took on me, not having a father in the house...the hole in your heart when you don't have a male figure in the home who can guide you and lead you. So I resolved many years ago that it was my obligation to break the cycle – that if I could be anything in life, I would be a good father."

True. An unfit, unresponsive, deadbeat dad may not be the person you want to seek out to have a close relationship with your son...I understand. But that doesn't mean that your child should be devoid of male contact or that you can't find a great male role model in your extended family, school, recreational park, sports venue, workplace, church, and more.

And what about you? Have you examined your upbringing? Of course, I assume that you're open-minded...at least enough so to be reading this book...but have you truly reflected on how you were raised? Were you brought up without a father? Or maybe you had a passive, unemotional father living at home, which is just like not having a father around? Or, did you lose your father early in life and never had a paternal model giving you insights on how to raise your son? Perhaps your ex-husband was abusive and that, too, affected your decision-making?

Whatever the reasons, I can't emphasize enough how important it is for a single mother to take a hard look at both her current and past situations involving men. You don't want to carry over negative patterns from a past relationship, or negative experiences that occurred with your parents, to the child you are rearing.

Here's an example of how past relationships can affect the present. One of the people interviewed for this book is a pastor who tragically lost his father as an infant. He discussed what it was like being raised by his mother while going through puberty:

"That was a horrible time. I didn't have any men I could talk to. My mother and I didn't have the TALK. When I was 8 years old she gave me a book called 'Where Did I Come From?' and said read this – that was it! That was the extent of our conversation. So when going through all those physical changes that happen to young men, I didn't know who to talk to about it. My maternal grandfather had been a womanizer when she was growing up and left her mother (my grandmother) with 10 kids to take care of. Her father was not a very nice person. From grandpa she got a distrust of men...and it was reinforced from my dad because he would go on weekend benders and they wouldn't see each other from Friday night to Monday morning. My mother wouldn't let me talk to my uncles because she felt like all her brothers had trouble with women and may have adopted his habits of womanizing and being abusive. But their relationships with women had nothing to do with their physical developments as men and what advice they could have shared with me."

The pastor was later asked if he missed having a male presence in his life:

"Oh yeah, I missed a male presence in my life. My mother was extremely overprotective and I recognize that much of it probably had to do with her being widowed when I was a baby and the problems I later had with epilepsy. Still, I liked sports like basketball and football and I think if I'd had a father figure in the house, I probably would have gotten to play on a team in high school because he would have debated with her and said – awww, let him play. I remember my urologist asked me because I'm a big guy, why didn't you ever play sports and I told him because of the seizures and he said to me high school coaches are trained for stuff like that. They know when to put you in and take you out. Hearing that seemed to justify many of the resentments I had later in life.

John P. Dennis

I particularly remember when I was 10, I didn't feel I had anyone on my side...that my mother would argue, and I didn't have a voice or anyone to go to bat for me. I think a father or father figure would have, or at least I hope would have explained to me what she meant or what she was trying to say to me...or just have him stand up for me at times."

What would he say to a single mother about raising a son?

"Learn the difference between protecting him and emasculating him. A boy has to learn how to be a man. I think my mom was right in one way – she could teach me how to treat a woman, but she couldn't teach me how to be a man."

Melissa Ludtke wrote in *On Our Own* that she spoke with many young men who did not have close relationships with their fathers...one never knew who his father was, and the others saw their fathers infrequently while they were growing up. All admitted that their father's absence created painful moments during their childhoods. One of the young men, who was a twenty-two-year-old father with a sixteen-month-old son and a one-month-old daughter stated: "I couldn't always go to my mom to talk about something. I felt uncomfortable going to her talking about sex. I needed Dad. It was like, 'Dad, yo, Dad. Where are you?' I ended up talking to my Unc."

Rodney Edison, a therapist, in an interview, talked about his sporadic relationship with his father and how he just needed to be around him:

"My parents got divorced when I was around five and my mother raised me and my younger brother. What I did know about my father was that he was kind of a street man that hung out on Avalon Blvd. When I was with him we would hang out at the barbershop, go to a bar, then to his bookie, and all these places on the same block. I never saw him that often. No regular or planned visits or activities were set up. It was more like my mother would make an announcement that I needed to see my Dad. Sometimes I would go over to where he stayed. He had a girlfriend and we all would hang out and watch TV. I remember my father shaving with one of those old shavers...lathering up. I remember standing in the bathroom watching him shaving and was fascinated.

As I grew older we never talked about girls or women or had that birds and bees conversation...didn't have it with my mother either. I kind of winged it, learned from others, pretended to know what people talked about, and basically grappled with it on my own. Yet, I did feel the need to be with my father at all costs...I didn't care what people thought about him. There was some part of me crying out why doesn't he call? Why doesn't he say I'm coming to get you, son? I felt like I needed to be around him even though we didn't have this great relationship. My mother was often angry and under a lot of pressure. I wanted to be around him simply because he was my father...

Officer J, a correctional officer out of North Carolina, had this to say about this prevalent attitude stemming from women who say 'I don't need anyone to help me raise my son':

"How can you say that you don't need any help? It's the same thing as me saying I don't need any help building this house and I'm aware I know nothing about building this house. I haven't been trained...I'm not a carpenter...I don't even know where to start! The best thing I can do is read books; educate myself on how to start the foundation. So I say that to say this: as a woman who knows nothing about being a man...you may know a lot about dealing with men, being in a relationship with men, but not actually being one...thinking like one...operating as a man...teaching a boy to be a man. How can you say, I don't need any help!

You have a generation of women trying to build and handle this complex thing called man without any instructions, without any teaching, without any tutoring.

Not too long ago a young lady that came to our church had 3 sons and her sons had lost their father. She entered the church and said, I'm at my wit's end, I don't know what to do...I pray that the Lord changes their hearts. One was in a gang, the younger one was following his brother's steps and he was starting to get involved in activity. When I heard her story I thought, I've worked in an environment where I've seen young men like this all the time in the system. I've got to get this kid before he does something stupid.

So I got him involved in a boxing club that trained kids for free and he turned out to be very good. I made myself available for the kid and I took classes too. I developed a relationship with him. I met with his mother and she would call me any time he was doing wrong...she might inform me that she had to put him out because he came home late or was smoking...so I would call him and ask where are you at? Are you going to class? I might see him walking and I'd pick him up and take him to training/practice. I'd pick up food for him and sometimes give him a little money to take his girlfriend out. And we'd spend time talking about girls. Some of these guys don't want their mom to know about what they're doing with girls. They might think she is going to get on them whereas a guy like me is going to give it to them real – No, I'm not going to validate you having sex without getting married – that's not what I'm going to do. And if you are, be smart about it; don't start getting these girls pregnant. I'm able to talk to them and deal with them on that level and it makes a big difference as opposed to them talking with their mom or a woman about it.

It was great to see a mother who was not afraid to say, I don't know what else I can do – somebody please help me. And it just took me standing up and other guys doing the same thing...something as simple as taking them to school...taking them to look for a job...taking them to eat...going to stores in the mall...and offering encouragement."

Officer J is a shining example of the men out there actively helping women who are willing to put their pride in their pocketbooks and ask for help if needed. To all single mothers, you may be the primary caregiver to your son because of the circumstances, but you don't have to do it alone – and you shouldn't. Boys need male role models in their lives; someone besides the mother that will give them attention, guidance, and good values, and show them what true manhood is all about. It's important to actively recruit male figures who you deem to have high esteem that can be found in your family, community, church, and athletic clubs; this can include uncles, grandfathers, cousins, friends, teachers, coaches, pastors, Big Brothers, etc.

I end this section with a quote by author Robert Bly that encapsulates the impact a mentor can have on a young man's life:

"In ordinary life, a mentor can guide a young man through various disciplines, helping to bring him out of boyhood into manhood; and that in turn is associated not with body building, but with building an emotional body capable of containing more than one sort of ecstasy."

Chapter Three

Mothers and Sons: He's NOT Your Husband, Lover, Best Friend, Nanny, or the Man of the House – He's Your Son!

Sweater, n.: garment worn by child when its mother is feeling chilly.

~Ambrose Bierce

What a great quote! Moms are constantly figuring out what their kids need. I can't remember how many times Mom reminded me to put on a coat before I went outside. She knew what I needed because she knew how I would feel after being outside for an extended amount of time. Fast forward twenty years and I realize after riding with my wife in the car that women have a completely different thermostat. Thank God for dual climate control in the newer vehicles. Because when I'm hot she's cold. I've come to the conclusion that men run a hotter temperature than women, or maybe it's all the jumping around. Moms have to make some assessments about their boys based upon what they themselves feel, and often it's not what the boy feels. In fact moms can be driven by loneliness, fears, insecurities and overreaching attachments to their sons.

In the documentary *No Greater Bond,* there is a very poignant moment in which one of the single mothers profiled talks about how difficult it was to accept that her boy had become an adult and to mentally "let go" of her attachment to him so he could move on, guilt free, and raise his own family. In a quivering voice and eyes brimming with tears, she admits that it was a struggle trying to reckon with, "He's my son, not my companion." She remembers that when her son had a baby with his girlfriend she became outraged, jumping up and down and screaming at him about making the decision to marry *that* girl. But Professor Jolene Swain, also featured in the documentary with her son, gave her friend a dose of tough love: "You cannot want your son to be at home with you and not with his girlfriend and baby...you raised him by yourself for the exact same reason and now you're getting ready to do it again?"

In the interview for this book Professor Swain elaborates on this point:

"The mother and son have to go through a healthy separation process. I truly believe at some level the mother-son bond is primal...I remember the first time a girl called the house my reaction was – what does SHE want? I wanted to scratch her eyes out! Later I'm saying to myself, what is wrong with me? Why did I emotionally react that way? But when other mothers don't understand that, they act on it, and play it out.

A lot of single mothers behave this way because of their socialization. And they don't want to hear about it because they are out there on their own doing it alone. The women totally shut down. The thought is, my son may have 2-3 kids with different women, but I'm letting him stay here with me...because maybe I'm not emotionally happy...my son makes me happy...and I will never embrace that woman he is with...I don't like her.

This is what I often hear from women instead of wanting to embrace the woman and trying to work with her.

I know it's frightening...but if you don't start the process of letting go when your son hits the age of 10 then at 15-18 when you're locked on, it becomes a problem. Boys raised by single mothers that get into trouble often have this rage and this rage at others is really directed at their mother – you made me a wimp! You didn't let go! On the inside I feel like a punk...I don't feel like a man!

From a theoretical standpoint I can explain how this young man feels, but not from an internal emotional point of view because I'm not a man. That's why he needs to talk to a man, so he can process his feelings. By not letting go women are committing a disservice to their son and to themselves. No mother wants her son not to live his life to full capacity. Ladies, you have to work on letting go...because letting go is love."

Here's another story told by an interview participant about the vibes he got from his mother and the grilling he received every time he went out on a date:

"It was difficult with my mother...even after I stayed home temporarily with her after graduating from college. If I was leaving to go out on a date she would state the ultimate buzzkill before I left – "Don't forget about AIDS!" She went there every time with stuff like this. If I came home at 2:00 or 3:00 in the morning she'd demand to know why I didn't call her. I'd answer, "I'm a grown man." Her response: "But you're in MY house!" The first time I had sex I walked in, looking a little disheveled, clothes messed up and she'd be sitting there with the light on – "What did you do? Did you have sex? Did you wear a condom?" My mother met a few of the women I dated when I was living at home and she hasn't met any since. She was always nice to them, but as soon as they left, I'd get a grilling about each one – I don't like her...she's too fat...she's too slow...there was always something wrong with them. Not once did I hear my mother say she liked someone I dated.

When I was growing up and interested in girls my mother would tell me – I'm a woman, too, so when you bring those girls some flowers, you bring me some too...and I'd think – really? – but I'm not dating you – I'm dating her! Honestly, I think there was a part of Mom that never wanted me to have anyone else in my life that might surpass her...I truly believe that."

It's no secret that mothers and sons have a special bond that goes beyond the psychological. A mother is the most influential person in a boy's life, particularly in the early years. Mothers are the primary caregivers to a child psychologically and emotionally starting from infancy. They make the first and most significant bond to a newborn that a man cannot possibly do. It can be a beautiful thing, but can also be destructive if a healthy separation process doesn't exist between the mother and son when he becomes a young man.

It's painful for mothers because they often feel that the child they bore is theirs. Letting go doesn't mean you love your son any less, it just means you're releasing him from dependency on you and you on him. The woman in the documentary is hardly alone in her unwillingness to let go of her son, strapping him to the invisible umbilical cord that keeps pulling him back to mama. This societal problem of single mothers not letting go of their sons when they reach a certain age continues to perpetuate itself from generation to generation.

This pattern is one of the main reasons why there is such a tremendous growth in single-parent families. Swain states that a mother should really say: "Uh, uh, you can't have a baby out there and live here! You should be with your family and if you're going to start a family you need to think about loyalty and commitment." Swain explains that the mother doesn't let go because her son is serving a purpose for her. He's her emotional support and may be her financial support...and as a result, we're setting up our sons to avoid going out and creating their own healthy families.

In his book *The Wonder of Boys*, renowned family therapist and author, Michael Gurian, discusses how much boys need love, attention, and a solid attachment to mom in the early stages of life from 0-10. But at the onset of puberty and adolescence when the boy's testosterone is raging wildly and making him feel crazed, he naturally begins to pull away. Mothers should be encouraging during this period and ready to transition him to his father, stepfather, and/or a positive male community ("village"). He points out that a mother who does not let go of her son may face the risk of her son growing up through adolescence resentful, rebellious, and wanting to punish her. And if not his mother, then the emotional dependency on his mother; unresolved issues may then cause continual problems in his relationships with girlfriends and spouses. These young men also mistakenly think that making a baby is the pathway from boyhood to manhood.

Gurian purports that most men today have been "underfathered" and "overmothered". He states the maternal style is based on the mother's sense of the child being hers – "she carried the child in her body, and the child seems like a part of her". The paternal style he describes as based on "the father's physical separateness from the child. In *The Invisible Presence*, Gurian recalls the troubled relationship he had with his mother and how it impacted him as a young man:

"My father was gone most of the time, so my mother had to do the bulk of the parenting. She and I developed a psychological connection by which I supplied her emotional nurturance in the absence of my father, as much as she supplied me the nurturance a child needed. She did not know how to let go of me nor I of her. As she and I tried to separate during my adolescence, so that my psychological clock could tick toward individuation and maturity, she became scared of losing me, and I felt guilty for leaving her. Meanwhile, I learned very little of a concrete nature from my father and other men about the spiritual and emotional life of men. Most of what I learned about women was confusing and still somehow stuck in relating to my mother. By the time I went to college I was still a boy, dressed in a man's body."

As you can see, a son's relationship with his mother affects the rest of his life - including how he interacts with, and the intimacies he shares with, the girls and women he encounters during his journey. That's why I stress emphatically to single mothers – he's not your Husband, Boyfriend, or Lover! Now you may think I'm being trite, or possibly offensive by bringing up the obvious...there's no way you would EVER think of your son as a boyfriend! But please let me clarify: I'm not speaking in a literal way or inferring there are any sexual no-no's occurring...I'm speaking psychologically and emotionally.

Gurian refers to it as "mother-son entanglement" and writes that it predominantly happens among adolescent boys and their mothers, and is often transferred onto lovers and wives after those boys turn into men.

"Both fathers and mothers turn to children to fulfill their needs when they don't believe their spouse is doing so. Statistically, it is more likely that a mother and son will become entangled...if anything, fathers tend to become more enmeshed with daughters...In emotionally unhealthy circumstances mothers form a lover relationship with an adolescent son. Some psychologists call this 'emotional incest'."

Jolene Swain states that most single moms have a very difficult time when their boy reaches adolescence.

"Boys start really feeling their oats...they get very powerful in the mothers' presence because they are coming into their own. Some of these moms get really scared and they don't know how to treat the boundaries. By the time these young men are 15 and 16 they might start going out there and making money and then bring it back into the house to help support the family. However, the mom starts to really lose a lot of power because now the son is in a role that he's not supposed to be in...so she really cannot get into setting the boundaries with him now that he's bringing money into the household, be it through drugs, working at 7-11...whatever...now he has too much power...and there may be no adult man there to keep him at bay. So this is what happens – now they've become this couple because they are really operating like a husband and wife in a sense, but obviously don't cross that boundary of a sexual relationship, so he goes out in the world and has sex, but he always comes back to his mama. The pattern has been set. That's why we're getting more single parents."

Contrary to this is a subject that is usually avoided in discussions about the mother-son relationship. Government and private studies from such sources as the *Handbook on Family Violence* and the *Journal of Social Work* report that boys tend more often to be the victim of physical and verbal abuse by a parent than girls; and ironically the parent most likely to physically abuse a boy is his mother. This fact may shock some of you, others not at all; but the main reasons cited for this trend is that mothers spend more time with their children than fathers do, thus giving them more of a chance to be abusive. Overstressed and frustrated single mothers, lacking support, find themselves having to discipline sometimes angry and unruly boys and end up being verbally and physically abusive to their sons.

This is a good time to examine another common phrase that is often and ceremoniously voiced on TV programs to young boys in single parent families. It starts out innocently enough with comments such as:

"Look at my little man!"

"You're going to have to look out for your family now!"

"He's the man of the house."

No he's not. He's your child!

Don't elevate your son to a position of "Man of the House" and then attempt to convince him that he suddenly needs to grow up and be prepared to take on the reins of an adult. It's not going to happen and you're setting him up for unnecessary and unreasonable psychological damage.

They seem like harmless statements or feel appropriate for the time being but in reality they put enormous pressure on the child if taken to heart, and they begin to shape his interest in assuming responsibility. By loading his mind with the burden of that excessive responsibility too early it contributes to the exact opposite result we see so often. It blossoms those boys into men that avoid responsibility, especially familial responsibility, and even job promotions, simply because they don't want to be responsible for others.

I've spoken to too many men who simply did not want to be the supervisor because they don't want to deal with being responsible for others. Aren't we quick to say MEN should be leaders, the heads of their families and a man's man? I hear guys applauded for being an alpha male but more often I hear stories of men avoiding their responsibilities or being slack in them. Let's examine a story:

Sam was a young teenager with a down-and-out Dad. Mom leaned on Sam to pay bills. She didn't care where the money came from and Sam felt so burdened to care for her that he turned to making money illegally. It wasn't just expenses Sam was covering; he even paid for his mother's hair appointments. She went to Sam for her needs instead of doing the extra it might take, or simply doing without.

Sam has taken on the obligation to provide for his mother. He's basically fulfilling the role of provider for her and can't distinguish between the parent/child and husband/wife relationship. This mindset will plague him into adulthood and ultimately strain any relationship he attempts to have. Professor Swain says mothers in these situations behave jealously towards their sons' spouses and expect them to accommodate their own needs above their wives'.

If Sam does marry he is destined to struggle with comprehending his roles and responsibilities, compared to healthy boundaries that are needed to diminish his mother's influence on him. A mother like this might use emotional blackmail to manipulate her son's feelings of sympathy for her. She's practiced it for years and the new wife is likely to spot it within seconds so she becomes an instant threat. To see an example like this reach its extreme let's look at Kay.

Kay works, pays his bills and is up and down when it comes to child support but some of that is associated with the recent recession. When

Kay's mother came up short for her house note Kay went behind on his rent and child support to pay his mother's bills. Is this odd or is it noble? Kay can't tell...his mother puts enormous pressure on him to help her out because he feels that he owes her for raising him. She's not above using a guilt trip if needed.

Kay is lost in a world that he cannot figure out. His baby's mother pursues him for child support which she needs to care for his son while he tries to ease his burden to care for his mother. The mom's inability to care for her own affairs reaches all the way into the life of her grandchild and deprives the grandchild of his needs. Kay's priorities are skewed. The umbilical cord is still attached but instead of nourishment flowing from the mother it is a suction pump that pulls resources from Kay and his child.

A Deputy Sheriff that has worked for the Department of Corrections in the jail and prison industry, has this to say about the pressures of being called the man of the house:

"I'm the oldest, and when our parents divorced I got thrown under the bus as becoming a bill payer and helping my mother to survive for my other siblings. She started stressing me out about bills that had to be paid; otherwise the utilities and other things would be turned off. Schoolwork was thrown on the backburner. At 13 or 14 I had the concerns of a grown man including cutting grass, bagging groceries, and walking to work. It was a huge shift when my father was no longer there. I remember the difference in how the bills were handled after the split and how weak and vulnerable my mom was. I would see her in an emotional state and how she would take it out on us...

At times I did feel like a big burden was thrown on me...when my mom used to cry on me. It just broke me all the way down. I didn't know if she was trying to manipulate me...but it gave me a guilt trip. I could never have anything...I need to put the family first. I couldn't have a new car or new clothes because I'd feel guilty and knew they had to come first. I was never really happy. When I had a girlfriend, I would buy her something, but I knew my family needed something. I always kept in my mind that they had the greater need. I eventually grew out of it...I knew it wasn't my calling to be the head of the household. I'm designed that way, but I didn't feel like I had earned the right at that stage...I was thrown into it."

In another interview a man spoke about how he felt, being dubbed the man of the house:

"Very early on I felt the pressure of being the man of the house and being responsible for my mother, especially emotionally because I knew financially I couldn't do anything for her. For example, I'll never forget when I was a teenager; the man she was seeing had a key to the house. My mother wasn't feeling good that day so when he opened the door and walked in I immediately went over to him and whispered, 'Mom's had a terrible day, so you might want to take it easy on her'. He replied, 'Thanks for letting me know,' and pretty much avoided her that evening. Over the years a lot of my mother's emotional stress I took on for myself. But what's interesting is, in retrospect, I kind of rebelled against her by not cleaning my room because I knew she was a neat freak and would get upset. That was my passive-aggressive way of getting back at her."

Permit your son to be a kid. Don't force adult pressures on him– no matter how difficult it may be for you – he's not ready. Don't rush him. Allow and encourage him to enjoy childhood and everything good about it. As you well know, it will be gone in a blink.

Sometimes an adult forgets the kid is not her NANNY and overwhelms him with all types of work and household responsibilities. There is nothing wrong with giving your son basic chores like emptying the trash or cutting the grass; small tasks that won't interfere with his schoolwork. I wholeheartedly endorse providing children with responsibilities but you must make an effort not to overload them with the worries of life at an early age. You can make the world of adulthood seem like a place he doesn't want to join because you put too much on him, and he only thinks the weight of that burden will grow. Let him be a kid with kid responsibilities as much as possible. Some things are inescapable and it should be understood that way. If you are the oldest you may have to watch your siblings until Mom gets home from work; but when you want to go play basketball or spend the night at your buddy's house, and you end up having to watch your siblings while Mom goes on a date, things are going down the wrong road. It would be easy for you to NOT want children later in life, or to feel like having kids are a burden.

Marcus is the oldest (15 yrs. old) and watches his little sister (8 yrs. old) after school until their mom gets home. When mom works late he cooks and might even put his sister to bed, depending upon just how late she is. Because of his mom's schedule and having a little sister, he isn't able to participate in after-school activities because he is needed to watch his sister. Most days when his mom gets home Marcus is on the porch talking with his buddies, since he can't leave until his mom gets there. When mom started dating she had Marcus watching his little sister all evening on the weekends.

We see the beginning of Marcus's frustration with watching his little sister. The line between helping out the family as needed is becoming blurred as mom transfers her own responsibility onto Marcus to watch his sister, while she dates and takes on more leisure activity - at the same time depriving Marcus. Work is a necessity and there is no way around it... Marcus can help out there. When it comes to leisure though, it's a good idea to start looking for options to hire a sitter or another family member to keep the little sister and allow Marcus his own leisure time.

Don't get me wrong; there are some benefits that may be realized from Marcus babysitting his sister. I've come across many young men who told me they knew they didn't want to have kids until they were married because of how much work it takes. Exposing your young man to child-care duties is helpful. However, I've seen the effect of too much child-rearing responsibility passed to the young guy that resulted in many men telling me they don't want kids at all because they just tie you down. They had to always watch their younger siblings growing up and they were glad to be done with that. It seems like what they really meant is: I don't want to be a father or married with children, because plenty of guys end up with children but are not involved in their lives.

And last but not least...HE IS NOT YOUR BEST FRIEND! Please don't share your relationship woes and financial troubles with your children. They are not your BEST FRIENDS! It places heaviness on kids that they can do nothing about, and creates worry in them. Your son will watch the men you are around over the years and grow to distrust relationships. Over time though, he will notice the faults that you bring to the table as well, and will begin to understand that much of the problem came from you; and since you are his number one point of reference for women, he will assume most or all women are like you. If you want to know what your son thinks of you then ask him what he thinks of women in general, and whether he wants to get married and have children.

Here's a good example of what I'm talking about that one of the interviewees shared about his experience:

"I recollect when I was around 10 or 11 my mother picking me up from school, and if she had a bad day at work she always talked to me about it. And if she needed to cry about things not going well in life...she cried to me about it. She placed a lot of emotional responsibility on my shoulders. If she were having problems with her boyfriend she'd pour her heart out to me so she wouldn't have to talk about it with him. I just had to sit there and listen. I didn't know what to do with it. I considered myself a smart nerdy kid and sometimes mature...but when I would act my age my mother would sometimes come to me and say, 'I don't know how to deal with you when you act your age'...Because to her I was always acting older."

Do you see what I'm talking about? What advice can your young son provide you? He's too easy for you to manipulate and he cannot give you honest or candid feedback because of the parent-child relationship. The worst part of this is that it will cause him to lose respect for you, and respect is a crucial part of society in the world of men. It starts with respect for authority, respect for others and respect for self.

Your son relies on you to take control, to be in charge, and to enforce the rules. Being a buddy and claiming to people your son is your best friend isn't going to cut it. It's okay to be friendly...but it has to end there. He'll have lots of friends in his lifetime, but only one Mom.

I hope you don't feel like I'm trying to diminish or take anything away from your relationship with your son. Yes, I may be asking you to disregard all those titles such as he's my best friend, companion, and man of the house...but for you the most important title, that still remains, and the one I want you to always lovingly embrace is:

HE'S MY SON!

John P. Dennis

Chapter 4

Where's My Daddy?

It is the same for all men. None of us can escape this shadow of the father, even if that shadow fills us with fear, even if it has no name or face. To be worthy of that man, to prove something to that man, to exorcise the memory of that man from every corner of our life – however it affects us, the shadow of that man cannot be denied.

Kent Nerburn, Author

I hadn't intended to handle this subject since it has so many dynamics, but after conferring with the many contributors it turned out to be a subject that warrants quite a bit of attention. Sooner or later the inevitable question will arise...some of you may have already encountered it, and I pray you handled it well. The question can be asked by your son at any age, or it might come at the most unexpected time during your daily routines – while you're in church, watching TV, mall shopping, driving the car, anxiously awaiting your new date to arrive, relaxing on the couch after a stressful day at work, or eating dinner. The question may vary on how it is phrased, but the content remains the same.

Where's my Daddy?

I can vividly remember praying that my mother and father would get back together after their divorce. Anytime I saw them interacting on civil terms I was hoping it was the beginning of them patching things back together. Even years later after my mom had remarried, when she divorced her 2nd husband my hopes that she would get back with my dad sprung right back. Young kids aren't really able to understand why their parents broke up and I'd wager that most really want a whole family. So what could I share that would be really helpful? I was only a kid myself so I'll address it from that vantage point.

Always tell the truth but share it in an age-appropriate manner. Does your 6-year-old really need to know that Mom or Dad cheated, or they were conceived from a wild night of partying? All I needed to know was that they didn't get along and couldn't live together. As I grew older more questions arose, and I received information that I could digest more easily at an older age. Of course there is no single approach that can explain this topic, since dads can be absent, incarcerated, alcoholics or just a rolling stone. If moms can find a way to always tell the truth though, it will make a difference.

What shouldn't happen is using a conversation with the kids to vent about dads. Personal interactions in the relationship shouldn't be shared with the kids. Remember - the kids' self-esteem and self-image are associated with their parents. If you say my Dad was a dog...I remember it. Later when Mom says, "you're just like your father," it will affect the boy. It affected me. Just keep in mind the young boy has a lot of questions that he only lets out over time to deal with the issues on his mind. In a way the questions he will ask about his father is a way of asking about his own identity.

There may be follow-up questions too, such as – Why doesn't my father live with us? Why did you guys split up? How come Dad never comes by that often? Do I have a father? Are you guys going to get married again? Can I live with Dad?

John P. Dennis

If the very thought of discussing your son's father, on account of a bitter breakup, instantly causes you to be angry or upset, then you may want to speak with a therapist/counselor, friends and family, or even write those feelings down first. Do whatever it takes to help curtail those emotions and seek objectivity before talking with your son about Dad. It's vital. Your negative emotions, no matter how warranted, should not be the backdrop for your son's own relationship with his father.

One respondent stated he was about 5 years old when he first asked what happened to his father. His mother told him his dad got sick and died when he was a baby. Not until he was an adult did she reveal the truth about his father suffering a tragic death. In fifth grade he again became cognizant of his father's absence and how it affected him.

"I remember going to my teacher after we had gotten back from summer vacation and all the boys were talking about what they did with their dad. It really hurt me because I didn't have that experience for summer. At lunchtime I asked the teacher, 'Do you think it's fair that all the boys talk about what they did with their dad and I don't have a dad?' She said, 'I understand what you're saying, but if you had a dad and there were things you guys did during the summer wouldn't you talk about him, too?' I agreed. It was one of the first times I was aware that there was supposed to be another parent in my life and there was not. I remember thinking since I don't have a dad...God was going to be my dad. And that was the first time I thought about a relationship with God because God was filling in for the father I didn't have."

Therapist Rodney Edison's experience was different in that his earliest memory prior to his parents' divorce is that they constantly argued. He rarely saw his dad. When the other kids talked about their fathers he insists that he was never jealous of them or felt like he was missing a dad, mainly because he knew where his father lived and did occasionally get to see him. He and his brother were so young that not having a dad around was just an accepted part of their lives. He recalls how he felt the last time he saw his dad:

"I remember going and seeing him in the hospital when it was discovered he had cancer. He had a lot of hair and I'd pick his hair out and rub stuff in it. It shocked me to see this big lump on his head...I kept massaging it hoping he'd feel better. I can't forget the weird look he gave me before I left. It was like he was trying to establish something at that point, but no words were spoken...it also showed how disconnected you can be. That same day he passed. He died in my early twenties.

At his funeral I felt guilty about not crying, especially after watching my mother and everyone else tearing up and wailing. I tried to force myself to cry and even mustered a few tears...but it wasn't real. I never had that connectedness or relationship with him.

The one thing Rodney maintained in the interview is that even though he sensed his mother's anger from their failed marriage, and that she appeared to carry that anger with her throughout her later relationships, she never spoke badly about her ex to the boys. Plus, she never prevented them from seeing their father whenever they wanted to. In fact, she encouraged it, despite her personal grievances with him.

Unfortunately, this is not the norm for many single mothers who steadfastly remain bitter from the fallout of a bad relationship. Quite often they do talk badly about the father to their sons and may even take it out on them, which is the worst thing you could do to your kids. It is likely that this will be used against you if your son feels anything you shared was untrue, or so biased that it is unreasonable. Kids can figure out later if they think you were trying to turn them against their other parent and will resent you for it.

I remember nit-picking everything negative I had ever heard about my Dad, trying to find out if it was true; and the things that I disputed became issues that upset me for awhile. No matter how badly your relationship (married or unmarried) ended, and no matter how excruciating it may have been, please try your best not to speak negatively about your son's father to him. Your reasons may be justified - he may be the consummate jerk, and you're further tempted to do so because he just hung up on you or never returns your calls...but don't go racing to your son and immediately launch into a tirade about his father (again, I'm focused on males raised by women in this book, but of course, this applies to girls, too!).

First of all, your son may have overheard your conversation after all the screaming and yelling, and now he's sweating internally prepared for you to come at him ranting about his father. He will feel like he has to assume some of the blame for his father's incompetence (according to you) because after all – it is his father!

For all you know he may already feel like it's his fault that his parents broke up because every time you start raging about his dad, he hears – your father doesn't do a damn thing for you, he left me as soon as you were born, he never gives me any money, he spends all his time with that WOMAN, he hasn't been a good father since you were born and never will be, and on and on it goes. The worst is when a mother negatively uses this expression to describe her son's recent behavior: "You act just like your father!" Suddenly the boy is thrust into a position he has no control over and wonders if he inherited some negative trait from his dad.

Be sensitive and realize you cannot allow your son to think that HE was in any way responsible for your divorce or breakup with his father. He may not understand the reasons you split up, and that's okay because he shouldn't be saddled with the particulars. More importantly, he needs to know that the demise of your relationship had nothing to do with him, and he needs to be assured he is still loved by both parents regardless of the situation. In the book, *Bay and Her Boys*: *Unexpected Lessons I learned as a (Single) Mom*, Bay Buchanan writes:

"Single parents need to constantly keep in mind – and impress upon their kids – that the divorce was not about them. Make it clear and repeat it often, like a mantra. From day one never let them think they had anything to do with this terrible upheaval in their lives. Tell them that their dad loves them, that nothing will change that – just as you love them and always will. This isn't a contest about who loves them more. Don't make it one.... your ex may not be so generous of spirit – don't respond in kind...this is really tough, but the key

is to remember that your concern is the kids...Your goal: do no harm. Don't demonize their dad. No blame, no harsh words, no tell-all tales. Divorce sent him out of your life...don't let it send him out of theirs."

It's so sad when a woman intentionally or unintentionally poisons her son's mind against his daddy due to a breakup, or to her ex not cohabitating with or marrying her. You must not share the dirty details of your divorce with your son – whether it's true or not; it's not fair to him. Your job is to protect him from all the ugliness that may have taken place. Save your vent for friends, family members, or a therapist.

Many women need to get rid of the mindset that going to a counselor or therapist is a sign of craziness – I see it more as a billboard illustrating how smart and caring you are to make an effort to surround your son with a reassuring emotional environment.

Here's that mantra: adult burdens and concerns should never be heaped on your son's shoulders. It shows a careless disregard for the emotional impact it may have on his psyche. When he gets older it may manifest itself terribly in other areas of your son's life. If your son hears you continually speaking derogatorily about his father and exclaiming all men are dogs, it affects his self-esteem and burgeoning manhood in untold ways.

If a boy is regularly exposed to his mother and her female friends endlessly excoriating men, then it may lead him to question whether any truly good, honorable, and decent men exist in the world; or if they are all fakes like his mother espouses. His mother's disapproval and condemnation of men ends up transforming into a self-fulfilling prophecy to her impressionable young man who starts engaging in self-destructive and criminal activities – dropping out of school, joining gangs, possibly facing imprisonment and being labeled another statistic.

Gillis Triplett in an online article entitled "10 Harmful Things Single Mothers Do To Ruin Their Sons Lives" writes:

"I constantly meet men who were turned against their biological father by their moms. I have listened to men tell how they thought about killing their dads or wanting to hurt him just to get even for being abandoned. In many cases, their dads did not abandon them. Some of these mothers refused to allow the child to interact with his father as a way to punish the boy's father. These mothers were plain evil by fueling poisonous lies of child abandonment."

On this same topic, Michael Gurian writes in *The Invisible Presence*:

"Most of the destructive messages a mother gives a son in relation to a disengaged father are messages that tear men and manhood down. These messages tear the male soul, and the son, as he grows up and realizes the male soul is his soul, hates men, doesn't trust men, and even becomes self-destructive, so powerfully can a father's absence and a mother's anger influence him. When his mother dislikes, hates, puts down, turns away from, does not respect men, and when the son remains, as he does in so many families in this culture, psychologically attached to and in collusion with her, how is he to grow beyond adolescence? What manhood is he to grow into?"

I want to be clear that I am not in any way absolving men of their responsibility to step up and be good men and fathers to their sons – there are a multitude of reasons, but no excuses, for both mothers and fathers to do their part in showering their children with complete devotion in raising them up to be healthy men and women. Unfortunately, many young mothers and fathers who came from single parent homes weren't given the proper skills to prepare them for the role of mother and father. Studies have shown that girls who grow up with one biological parent, ordinarily the mother, have a higher probability of becoming teenage moms than those with both parents. This includes teenage boys becoming fathers with no intention of marrying the mother of their child.

Ludtke in *On Our Own* writes:

"The measures researchers use don't address the gut-wrenching moments of everyday life when children want to know about 'Daddy' or wish they had one, or when fathers try to figure out how to fit into families when they have

no model to show them how, or when mothers and fathers try to reconcile their mutual anger and distrust with their desire that their children be close to both parents."

The point here is, don't let your emotional anger or bitterness overrule your logic when it comes to the betterment of your son. It's not about you – it's about him! I understand if the father of your son is physically and/or emotionally dangerous or could potentially put your child's life in jeopardy because he's a substance abuser that refuses to seek help. But don't shut the father of your child completely out of his life because YOUR relationship with him deteriorated.

There is not enough emphasis placed on dad being a part of his son's life and contributing to his emotional support as well. Society expects the father to support their children financially, and rightly so, but not enough pressure is put on fathers to be more a part of their kids' lives. That's why President Obama's appeal to fathers to be fathers and step up was so important. Nonetheless, this applies to mothers, too, to help fathers meet their obligations by encouraging them, opening their arms to them (as difficult as it may be) to co-parent and help bring up their son.

Make an effort to point out the positive traits of your son's father and how that reminds you of him. Let him drop the kid off at school, let him take part in parent-teacher meetings, invite him to see his son take his first steps, let him be at the birthday parties, let him warm up the infant bottle, and so forth. And try to do so, as painstaking as it may be, without showing the hurt on your face – because your son will notice. Don't let your calls to dad on behalf of your son always be about money.

I'm talking about good men, fathers who sincerely want to be in their son's world, but may have been blocked because of a mother's own personal beef with dad that has no bearing on their son. Even if a man can't provide much financial support, don't cast him away strictly because of that. Men have to understand and appreciate that their benefits as a father to their son transcends the financials.

Too frequently men keep their distance from their children because of embarrassment, and viewing themselves as inadequate parents due to lack of financial resources. You have to keep in mind – men define themselves by the amount of money they make, and a lack of income is usually linked to a loss of manhood to many men. And it doesn't help when the ex chastises and punishes him by selfishly attempting, in every conceivable way, to prevent him from seeing his son unless he comes up with some bucks.

That doesn't resolve the son's need to be around his father, nor does it incline the father to be more involved in his son's life. Even without a sufficient income a dad can serve as a powerful and positive influence to his boy – just by being around and showing his love. Oftentimes, particularly in the case of young fathers, they haven't been given the tools to help them construct a relationship with their son. They won't learn how wonderful their child is and the joys of being a father if they are prevented from any contact and communication because the mother is being territorial. A single mother must give her son the opportunity to have a great relationship with his father; you've seen all the stats – too much is at stake to ignore it in the child's upbringing. Let him see his father as often as possible.

Correctional Officer J, states that many guys in prison have kids that were babies when they were first incarcerated. The only things the kids know about their dads are through visits and communication via letters and emails. Once they have served their mandatory sentence it's often the first time the father will have an opportunity to be with his child. Ferrari feels it's never too late for a father to still try and build a relationship with his offspring. He remarks:

"For that mother, decide what's important – you and their father's relationship or allowing a relationship to kindle that can set the tone of that child's life you brought into the world. Because as parents, we live our lives...a lot of people have their kids young...but once you bring a life into the world, you are no longer the concern – your concern is that child, that life. As a mother

you must establish that relationship with the father, that connection...and if the father doesn't want to be a part of that, you can't make them do that...I understand...but you can lean on someone that's close, like a grandfather. Find a male, somebody...you can't tell me that there's nobody that will step in and help out."

Your son must be free to love his dad. If all those bad things you want to say about his father are true – let him find out for himself through his episodes with dad and come to his own conclusions. Let him vent to you about it if need be; without you interjecting your biased thoughts. Ultimately he'll respect and appreciate you more for your objectivity during those trying times.

If his father is truly a "Dad Risk" for all of the negative reasons I outlined earlier (substance and/or physical abuse), then search for some wonderful male role models to fill the gaps – call on the male community...the village. With help and guidance a boy might be able to adjust without his father, but he still needs men in his life.

Chapter Five

"A man is at his youngest when he thinks he is a man, not yet realizing that his actions must show it."

Mary Renault, "The King Must Die"

A Man Without A Model

"I'm a grown-ass man! I don't have to listen to you! Nobody tells me what to do! I'll do whatever the hell I want to do! You ain't my Mama or Daddy!"

I apologize for the profanity but the quotes are accurate. I've heard many young men erupt into this kind of tirade for a variety of reasons, but usually when they're in conflict with an authority figure. It's always perplexing to me why someone feels the need to declare his manhood with, "I'm a grown-ass man!"

Let's examine a story about Wesley…

Wesley had been in basic training for about 2 weeks now and it was in full gear. Up early every day, running, getting yelled at, push-ups, getting yelled at, cleaning and getting yelled at some more was the daily routine in BMT. The Drill Sergeant decided to pick squad leaders to supervise sections of the entire platoon. Wesley was not selected but that didn't matter much to him. He didn't want to be responsible for anyone else anyway.

One morning Wes was running behind trying to get downstairs for the morning formation. Arriving late was not really an option and his squad leader knew that he would take the blame so he was standing at the door yelling, "hurry up" to the last few trainees. Wes was hustling and finally got his stuff together and headed out…as he came up to the squad leader the young man yelled again…"Hurry up private!" Wes stopped and stared him in the face then barked back…"You don't yell at me…I'm a grown-ass man!"

The squad leader stood motionless and somewhat confused. Wes went down to formation feeling vindicated.

Wes is declaring he is a man. He felt disrespected by the yelling and has decided that people he does not respect will hear from him. Respect is earned and that squad leader had not earned Wesley's respect. Wes has adopted a street version of respect where strength or force allows you to demand respect. He didn't learn it at home. At home Wes got accustomed to his mom and her feminine methods of dealing with confrontation. Wes never learned some of the common ways of the world and the way authority works. The squad leader had positional authority over his given responsibilities. Since Wes never learned about positional authority he is confused about how to relate in a military environment.

Although serving in the military is not for everyone, I've come across many young men who could have used that avenue as a course to change their life. Some of those guys told me squarely "I don't like people telling me what to do." It's a statement that is very telling and very crippling. Where can you find a job that doesn't have supervisors and managers who tell you what to do? So we can expect these young men to struggle in the workplace as they try to deal with the realities of the world.

Wes shows us a few other things as well. He is explaining to us that he feels the squad leader is speaking to him as if he were a child, or in a manner that is not respectful to him. Wes is not sure what really being a man is and so he makes sure that he reinforces it with his emotional outburst. It's important not to confuse Wesley's emotional response with being feminine.

When he finds fault with authority he determines that he does not need to respect them. Everyone must earn his respect. Mom created this when she continually talked down about his father to the extent that he finally lost all respect for his dad. The bleed-over effect however, is that he might extend this mental processing to all other settings where respect is assumed, such as towards school officials, police officers and even supervisors on his job.

These young men are not just bark with no bite. In a way different from women, they are willing to get violent to prove to you that you are dealing with a man, because they are willing to fight for their respect. Since they don't have a good model in their mind regarding the role of manhood they have settled with the law of the jungle. An MRW is always unsure of his manhood and is always trying to prove it when he feels disrespected. Instead of maturely diffusing the situation or ignoring it, you might find an MRW ready to escalate the situation into something you don't want to deal with.

In the book, *Boys to Men: Maps for the Journey*, Gregalan Williams discusses how his mother raised him on her own and was a "teacher, protector, provider, and primary companion" for him. Yet, as he reached high school he chose "to ignore the map of my own experience." Suddenly he started calling women, who he used to profess respect for, "ho's".

"I ignored the truth of my own experience because somewhere in my head I mistakenly believed that term and other derogatory terms like it

were passwords that would get me into the secret clubhouse of manhood... Gentlemen, lots of us have been reared and are being reared by women. For years we've depended on them for our very lives...I perpetuated a bad thing in our culture, first in my speech, then, eventually, with my attitude...

Maybe that's part of the reason we're always so quick to fight when somebody talks about our mom or our sister...Could it be that somewhere inside we know that we have disrespected our own mothers and sisters when we disrespected other men's mothers, sisters, and daughters...That when we slap that other guy we slap him partly to slap the guilt out of our own heads?"

Interestingly enough, one of the greatest insults in this sub-culture is to call a guy a "Bitch". It could have many connotations, but referenced against this backdrop of men being raised by women, somehow they identify weaknesses among each other and consider those attributes very distasteful. What may be even worse though is that the behavior of name-calling and verbal abuse as part of an emotional explosion is probably something you'd get from mom, as compared to dad. Guys certainly pick on other guys, but anyone who knows girls knows that they go for the brutal attack laced with some kind of truth which makes it sting that much greater. When guys razz another guy they expect him to "man-up" and be able to take it without getting his feelings hurt. Women are different...they are purposely trying to hurt your feelings when they verbally bash at you. MRWs have picked up this attribute as well.

He learned that emotional overreaction from mom or from the other MRWs he hangs around with. The influence of other MRWs on the playground cannot be ignored as a major issue. When the young teen is confronted with a problem at the basketball court the situation can easily escalate based purely on his friends. If his friends break it up and tell him to calm down because "it's just a game", it allows for a very different outcome than if they tell him not to let that dude disrespect him. The level of self-respect is not developed in these young men so they are insecure and easily influenced.

Rodney Edison, in discussing his upbringing, reflects on how his mother's primary emotions were frustration and anger:

"She established a style, a tone, for how we learned to handle things, I think my brother even more so than me...he is very critical and high strung and that's how my mom is. My wife says I took on that person too and that I'm hypercritical and not aware of it. I would approach people who didn't do things the way I saw it and sometimes be overly critical and not having the empathy... that's why I think I drifted into psychology...I was learning about myself on an unconscious level. People say I'm so empathic. I also see now how much my mother sacrificed...she was under the gun a lot...sometimes I can't believe it. It was through the organizations (i.e. boy scouts, sports) that I learned my "manliness" .... I wouldn't let anybody punk me, but I don't feel like I had to overcompensate by getting into fights. My brother took on more of my mother's personality type and he had nobody to bounce it off of – that was the model he took more of the traits from...he'd pop off faster.

I'd say both my brother and I are more emotionally driven...and I think that does have a lot to do with my mom because she was an emotional person and less logical or intellectual about her emotions. That's how we learned to handle adversity...it became our style. On that level it's more of a womanly thing...that makes more sense to me and characteristic of women. I can remember asking my mom, why are you so upset? Why do you have to take it to that level? It was baffling to me. It was at the drop of a hat sometimes. My brother took on that persona about situations that didn't seem to call for it. A lot of times it wasn't that serious...from my frame of reference he seemed like he was a frustrated angry person. I remember getting into a thing with my mother and he'd look at me like you shouldn't talk to our mother like that – he would immediately take her side. It was like he became the man of the house when I came back from school after being gone for several years. Any disagreement my mother and I had he'd jump to her defense, making me the rebel and bad guy."

According to Officer J, fear also plays a role in how a guy reacts to conflict:

"When these guys join a gang, they do it for protection, out of fear...fear of being different...and a lot of those guys can shoot, but they can't fight...I've been doing this for a long time...I have had to go one on one with a lot of dudes and I'll expose them...you may have done murder, but you can't fight...they don't even know how to take a punch or throw a punch. Picking up a gun because you are fearful...you were raised by that woman, but you've never been taught how to square up, how to take one...these guys they will pick up a gun quick because they are emotional and when you have a male that's emotional he becomes dangerous...an emotional male is a dangerous thing because his rage can be vengeful...an angry woman might cut your tires up...you have some women that might kill you, but an angry man who wants to get past that point is emotional and doesn't realize the repercussions or the consequences of what he is doing is very dangerous. And when I've talked to these guys after they've done their time and all they say, 'Man, I have never done anything like that before, and the guy was just running off at the mouth and I just blanked'...This guy has not learned how to handle his emotions, he hasn't been taught how to think rationally, your emotions conquer you.

Officer T has a similar take on how males raised in fatherless homes often find it difficult to deal with people in authority:

"At that time when I was growing up, some of my friends had never seen their dad. All of them had this problem with authority. If you've got a problem with authority, right away that will run you into law enforcement and possibly the prison system. The father figure is that authority figure. Right away you recognize that you're not running anything and somebody else is running things...you know what I'm saying...they're going to delegate authority...so once you are confident enough you can make decisions on your own. It's like a four-legged stand...you can't pull out one of the legs and expect it to stand up...so he gave us sensibility and an understanding of responsibility. In the hood people will say, when you are working for the white man you are a sucker...when you're working for your dad; you're working because it's the responsible thing to do. If you want something...he'll take you to go and get it and show you how to get it...there's no other trickery.

Working with my dad, things were explained to me in more detail. He taught me that a job is how you get the seed money to get things you want and how to do things such as starting your own business and/or getting other things that you want like a house, car, etc. He talked about how not to put everything on your back, how to save money and put some back in for future needs. Even when I was in the prison system, I used to talk to the young black men and I would tell them how much stronger I am than you...I'm built stronger than you because I was raised from my dad, my granddad, and his dad; I have all their wisdom poured into me. As a result, I've got years of wisdom in me.

Many females are like these guys in prison and tend to become more emotional. During the visitations I'd see a number of females, but very few dads came to visit. I'd hear lots of complaining as they explained things to their mothers...it's different when you have a man in the picture...you have to deal with an authority figure."

Officer T's experience working with MRWs in prison was similar to Officer J's in that he also dealt with highly emotional men who felt disrespected:

"They tend to be more emotional, more combative, unreasonable, they're putting it on the line...if it was more typical of having a dad you'd say that ain't worth fighting for...let him have it...if he wants it that bad, let it go...they stole from you, it ain't worth the battle...they are on this somebody's testing them, disrespecting them and all the other stuff...if you find somebody is disrespecting you, does that mean you feel somebody has to fear you? To them it means, if you disrespect me, you have to fear me. 90% of the fights I go through it's always because someone says 'he disrespected me' – so I say to them 'so you're telling me since he disrespected you, he now has to fear you'?! Is disrespect a sign of fear? Does that word mean you need to fear me?

With a dad you don't have to go into all that stuff about you need to fear me...So there's some kind of breakdown in communication. So you take these guys and they design their own system in the prison without a male presence and they translate it back into the street...they put that same code back on the street like no snitching...so they run a whole system...remember, he had to sell drugs to take care of his family...so he ends up developing the code of a drug dealer...so he goes to prison, he comes back out on the street and now he tries to control the whole block – socioeconomic power – and now the police try to straighten stuff out, but now they can't do anything...now they're running the prison rules on the street...and making sure no one can snitch...again, you're disrespecting me – you need to fear me."

My last word on the "I'm a Grown-Ass Man" syndrome is that this phrase can also be instigated by a mother's dating behavior. A mother should never expose her son to a revolving door of different males she's seeing. If a single mother is dating then she should do so when her son is at his dad's place or with a family member or friend. If a woman is truly ready to invest in a long-term relationship then a new man can be eased into the boy's life. Letting your son see a variety of men frequently traipsing in and out of your life because of your own needs flings the door open for your son to disrespect and devalue women.

Gillis Triplett powerfully states in his article the things single mothers can do to ruin their son's lives when they date irresponsibly:

"As he witnesses your failed relationships, tears of regret from your manifold sexual liaisons and learns how you were dumped, played, dismissed and disgraced at the hands of detestable males, his conscience becomes desensitized to the well being of all women."

Thus, this dysfunctional frame of mind will lead him to once again swagger and crow: "I'm a grown-ass man...I know everything I need to know about women – you can't tell me nothing!"

Consequently, an often unnoticed side effect and fallout of being raised as an MRW is the deep unnatural insight these men learn on how to manipulate relationships with women. While it is hard for them to maintain a healthy relationship, it is a relatively easy thing for them to seduce and discard women with uncanny skill. In the years of watching their mother navigate relationships, and conferring with other guys in the same family structure, these guys all tap into the very potent philosophy that often captures women without them even knowing he is gaming.

I believe the guys are somewhat oblivious to it as well and this accounts for the large numbers of women that get tangled up with men who are not decent, law-abiding or even considered a good catch. These men can be going nowhere in life and still catch a decent lady in a relationship by deploying a tactic I refer to as "THE POST-DATED CHECK."

Warrick knows the game. He's been to jail a few times for child support and once for a domestic issue. His record bars him from getting better jobs so he's stuck for the most part in the "hustling" system of cutting grass, handyman work and doing odd jobs for people. It's good that he works but he can't afford a stable living so he lives with his mother until he can get "back on his feet". Warrick met Shirley at a house party and when she saw how he was dressed, his swagger and cool lean it caught her attention. A little time behind bars, long days on the b-ball court and labor jobs also equal a physique that most ladies call fine. And Warrick knows how to dress as most MRWs do. Shirley sees Warrick in a totally different light than men would see him. Warrick told her he can't work for people on that 9 to 5 grind because he's got real dreams of starting his own business. He's an entrepreneur and when a few key components line up he will be set to take off. He told her that she's just the type of woman a man like him had to have because successful men have to have a certain kind of woman at his side.

What is THE POST-DATED CHECK? It's just what it sounds like. I don't have the money in my account yet...but I get paid next Friday so here is a check dated for next Friday that you can cash in on later when I get the money in the bank. It relays a few messages.

1. I'm ready to commit right now...uhhh but I can't. But to show you how serious I am about this deal...here is a check.

2. I'm working at it...in other words: I have all kinds of potential and it's about to come to a head. It's as good as money in the bank.

3. I trust you. So hold this for me. I realize you could damage me by trying to cash this too early but I believe you are a person that will do right by me.

All 3 of these concepts when viewed in a relationship context explain that this man is clued in on one of the number one attractants to women---ANTICIPATION. She's got to have it and if you can stir it up in her she'll be thinking of you even when you are not around, and that's how he gets the girls over and over again – with empty promises. She wants to believe...

This kind of MRW has become a master manipulator. Even though I've met woman after woman with a fantastic list of qualities they desired in a man, they always seemed to get hooked up with men like Warrick. Don't expose your son to your relationship woes and, in the process, plant the seeds of a master manipulator.

Keep in mind, too, if you're dating, especially in the event of divorce where your son knows enough about his father to appreciate him, that the boy's initial alliance is going to be with his dad, regardless of whether you like his father or have disdain for his behavior. That is his male attachment, and he might be angry at you in some sense for pushing his father away – whether he's right or wrong in that assessment. As Michael Gurian asserts in *The Wonder of Boys*:

"Boys often idealize divorced, even distant fathers, as much as they feel anger and pain about the father's physical, geographical, or emotional separation. Boys will rarely see a new man as capable of being the ideal father they have in their minds, and thus will most often be unable to risk attachment to a new man. Their attachment to dad led to profound trauma when he left or was forced away from them."

It's a difficult leap for a young boy to attach to a new male in the picture, so I would advise you to choose wisely who you bring around your son, because if he rejects the role models you introduce he is much more likely to be shaped by outside pressures.

Consider this interview with a former prison guard...

"Not to disrespect any mothers or to diminish all the hard work they have done but at a minimum someone needs to consider the reality of the many guys in the prison system. They were almost all raised in single-parented homes by their mothers. Does that mean anything? I've known guys and gals that were raised by their fathers. They don't go to jail...they had manners and they had a work ethic. They might be a little more hard-core about stuff but it seems to me that men raise children better than women, at least where it comes down to being a productive member of society."

I wasn't sure about that assumption so I did a little research and the statistics are worse than I imagined. An article on Fathermag.com cited 85% of all youths sitting in prisons grew up in a fatherless home (Source: Fulton Co. Georgia jail populations, Texas Dept. of Corrections 1992). What an incredible perspective! I must admit that I've never heard this take on parenting; yet as I recalled the few people I've known who were raised only by their fathers, each and every one of them was doing okay. A few of the females that I knew were a little on the tough side and might be more balanced out by developing their domestic side, but that's not necessarily a negative trait.

What can we glean from this very interesting insight into male parenting? Moms need help from the men! Males appear to be effective in their role protecting the family and giving advice to help the kids safeguard their lives. They also help kids fit into society at large, teaching them the written and unwritten rules that make all the difference.

When it comes to boys, who else can give young boys the example they need to see? I recall watching my dad repair a mower when I was around 5 years old. It had begun to sputter and he mentioned something about the carburetor. He unscrewed a part of the mower and then pulled out what looked like a sponge to me. Next he cleaned the sponge and then dropped a little gasoline inside. He put it all back together and started that mower. Fast-forward 20 years later and I'm outside mowing my lawn when my mower begins to sputter. I instinctively took the same steps I'd seen my dad take before. My mower started just like his and I noticed my 6-year-old son watching me like a hawk. I don't even know if that's the correct method to repair that specific malfunction in a mower or if it's just a patch job; but what I do know is that young boys are constantly absorbing from the men around them. They take in lessons by teaching and by examples, whether you are teaching them deliberately or not. They need to get a solid understanding of what it means to be a man and when they have reached manhood. And I can't emphasize this enough – teach your son good morals and values, but let him express his feelings in his own manly style - do not pressure him to present those feelings in your way of conversing.

Previously I discussed how mothers should not catapult their sons into being the man of the house. On the other hand I find that the side effect of men raised by mothers is that many of them, once they reach adulthood, don't care about being the head of their own house.

During his interview Rodney Edison stated:

"Because my father was not around, I never had that posture about being the breadwinner...the man of the house...I don't feel I needed to be that man or make more money than my wife. A lot of women want the guy to be that way and that's not me. My wife and I have had that conversation...it's part of my making...and I've never been threatened by a strong woman."

It can be his wife, it can be his girlfriend, it can be his mom, and it can be his wife's mom, just as long as it's not him. Taking on the whole responsibility of a wife or kids is a big undertaking and MRWs are usually accustomed to seeing women shoulder most of the burden in the family. For whatever reason, since their dad was not around they don't have that inherited tendency to take charge, take responsibility and lead. They grew up in a matriarchal structure so they may even be attracted to more dominant women, to whom they are more comfortable relating.

We don't touch upon it in this book but the young girls growing up with just their mom tend to develop into responsible adults who are uncomfortable letting a man lead in the home, or depending on him for their well-being. This makes for a neat match-up with the guy who doesn't want to take his place as the leader in the family...except it's not the way he's made and over time after that detachment from his mother he will still drift towards his natural masculine tendency and the partner in the house will often struggle with him over power issues. You will end up with an individual that wants the power and respect of manhood but not the responsibilities that go along with it.

Lastly, there are a couple of other things I'd like to discuss before ending this chapter on MRWs starting with – GOSSIP! How do MRWs know that 50 Cent had a beef with Lil Boosie and Jay Z cheated on Beyoncé with Mya? A whole male culture for gossip has been created to the extent that there are now male-focused gossip magazines.

Too many of our young men are growing up insecure about themselves. While parents might be the number one avenue to build a healthy sense of security and self-respect in a child, gossip is surely one of the top assailants trying to destroy that child's self-image. Children start at a very young age saying mean things about one another and passing it around at school. Sometimes no matter how hard Mom or Dad has tried to convince their child that what they are wearing looks just fine, a mere snicker by a crowd of kids can undermine any confidence kids have about their appearance. It's difficult for kids who have a stable and secure home front to deal with gossip, let alone our MRWs. So here is how it plays out.

It might be fair to say that the larger group engaged in gossip is women, and if young Johnny hears mom gossiping all the time he'll get the gist of how it goes. No matter what she tries to tell him about not worrying what others say, subconsciously he'll still know that gossipers mock you, make fun of your clothing and even poke fun at your family.

If he hears it at home it only makes it worse because at its heart gossip also gets used as a manipulation. Once he feels like he's got to have the latest Jordans or the newest gear and even hang with a certain group, that youngster gets lost in the crowd. He'll be overly concerned with what others think about him, how he looks and whether he is being talked about. Insecurity will undermine his manhood and make him a follower instead of a leader. If he is desperately concerned with just fitting in it could get really hard to manage his conduct when he hits the teen years and the voice with the strongest persuasion in his life starts shaping his behavior. The battery of gossip starts changing and emphasizing what the kids consider important. Eventually the MRW starts focusing on clothing and appearance in a manner more like a woman than a man.

Men who have focused on fashion and their appearance to such a great extent have captured an entire category and gained the label of "Metrosexual". Wikipedia defines it as: "a man who is especially meticulous about his grooming and appearance, typically spending a significant amount of time and money on shopping as part of this." They worry about clothes and their appearance, and can be found paying for someone else to cut their grass, paint their house, wash their car or change their oil. Maybe that's a little harsh on the metros or an exaggeration of the definition... it's just an opinion, but I bet you he wouldn't throw away his collection of Jordan shoes!

Women like MRWs, but it's hard for them to maintain a long-term relationship because metro MRWs can't fulfill other needed components in a relationship that balance out the couple. After a time women read the behavior as feminine when he is "primping" in the mirror.

Often I hear single mothers boast to their friends that their son is so much more sensitive and understanding about women than boys raised with their fathers in the house. Again, don't fool yourself into thinking a boy is better off in some way without a father figure in his life. That's finding an excuse for not making a concerted effort to bring more male role models into his life – or just not seeing his needs; and for you it's a matter of convenience to let him hang out with you and your women friends. A boy can be just as sensitive, understanding, and more insightful with a father or male presence. I mention insightful because he has the opportunity to observe both male and female role models. I view it as a given that a boy should be raised to respect the qualities they can emulate in both men and women without losing their masculinity.

The real question is: have you mistaken or masked his abundance of sensitivity for being overly protected and overly smothered with affection? Have you performed the tougher job of loosening the apron strings?

Don Elium and Jeanne Elium discuss in their book *Raising A Son: Parents and the Making of a Healthy Family* the issue of mother-guilt and overcompensation:

"It is not surprising that mothers feel frustrated and confused about how to parent a son. Mother bashing (the syndrome of 'let's blame everything on Mom' because she was too engulfing) has become as popular as putting all of the blame on fathers for their absence. Part of the truth for many mothers and sons is that, because the father was either absent at work or absent altogether, the mother overcompensated out of necessity – she had to be THE parent. Many single moms have performed admirably under these circumstances but have failed to provide what their sons needed at certain ages, because mothers make lousy fathers. When mothers must overcompensate for the lack of fathers, sons will be unable to get in touch with their own deep masculinity."

Once again I make that clarion call to you. You must work hard not to be the overprotective and smothering parent that impedes a son's normal development. As he gets older don't let him be dependent on you, or you on him, for his emotional fulfillment. Yes, in the early stages it's essential for him to bond with his mother and develop that trust that will last a lifetime. But he must separate from his caregivers (including the father) and feel his own power and independence.

No worries. He will always love you and you'll gain a healthy individual in the process.z

John P. Dennis

Chapter Six

The Societal Forces and Pressures Confronting Your Son

"It is easier to build strong children than to repair broken men."

Frederick Douglass

If you envision the eagle pushing the young eagles out of the nest prompting them to fly it draws up an image embodying that philosophy. As parents, our greatest wish is to see our children leave the nest as resolute, capable, and stable-minded adults who become productive members of our society. Notwithstanding our hopes, children today are reluctant to step out into the world and establish themselves. There are many factors out there, such as an economy that prevents a successful launch for our kids in assuming their independence and charting their own path – particularly for the males.

This does not preclude that young women don't face similar obstacles or carry their own unique set of issues, but my focus in this book is on the problems and barriers exclusive to young men. It is vital that single mothers are alert to the social forces affecting our sons in order to better enable them to successfully transition to manhood and provide them help so they can navigate society's rocky terrain.

Civil rights attorney Lisa Bloom, in her book *Swagger*, goes in-depth about the societal forces aligned against boys. She states in this excerpt:

"Ensnared by these four powerful forces – failing schools, an unwelcoming economy, thug culture, and a harshly punitive justice system – more boys and young men than ever are on the sidelines, cut out of a middle-class life, scratching their heads as to how that happened. Although women and girls suffer under these conditions too, there's no question that, on the whole, these forces disproportionately hammer our boys."

Bloom contends that the old-school way of thinking – that once teens or twenty-somethings are out of school, they should by all accounts be able to land an entry-level starter job, in which they can get their foot inside the door, be industrious, and climb up the corporate ladder as the years go by, is out of touch with reality. She claims that 55% of our youth are not working and some have either stayed in school or gone back to school while hoping for an improvement in the job market.

According to the unemployment rates for young people (ages 16-24) reported by the U.S. Bureau of Labor Statistics, the number of unemployed youth was 3.4 million in July 2014. The Bureau states that among major demographic groups, July unemployment rates for young men were 15.1%, young women 13.4%, whites 12.2%, blacks 24.8%, Asians 10.9%, and Hispanics 16.5%.

The *Tavis Smiley Show* on PBS presents this "Fact Sheet" report:

- *In general, 6.2 million young people were high school dropouts in 2007.*

- *Only 14% of African American eighth graders score at or above the proficient level. This reveals that millions of young people fail to understand or evaluate text, provide relevant details, or support inferences about the written documents they read.*

The Congressional Black Caucus Foundation (CBCF) espouses in its report that the situation for Black males in the United States is tenuous.

"Although 45 percent of Black males who are 25 and older have attempted college, only 16 percent have a four-year degree, which is half the percentage of White males who have a four-year degree. Black males are incarcerated at a rate that is 7 times the rate for White males and are more likely than any other race group to be a victim of a violent crime, including homicide....

Notwithstanding, Black males enroll in college at a rate that is comparable to White males, despite the fact that the high school dropout rate for Black males is twice as high as the dropout rate for White males. In fact, if all 1.1 million Black males who are currently enrolled in undergraduate programs eventually graduated, the total number of Black males with college degrees would increase by 71 percent, nearly achieving parity with White males. However, college completion rates among Black males are dismal, particularly at community colleges and for-profit universities...

We need to move beyond merely getting Black males into college. We need proactive strategies to prepare them to compete at a university that has a record of retaining and graduating Black males. Too often, Black males with respectable high school academic records are shoveled off to community colleges, which generally have very low completion rates. Today, of the 1.1 million Black males enrolled in college, more than 529,000 (42.8 percent) are attending community colleges, compared to only 11 percent who attend Historically Black Colleges and Universities (HBCUs). Another 11 percent of Black males attend for-profit universities such as the University of Phoenix, which as a single institution enrolls the largest number of Black males in the nation."

Even though the above statistics concentrate more on the abject plight facing people of color in the educational system, in general, males of all races are dealing with an educational system that is not catering to their needs in modern society, nor acknowledging the many distractions that are affecting them. Bloom expounds upon the fact that girls are outperforming boys in every grade and subject. She writes that boys are "medicated, disciplined, suspended, and expelled far more often than girls are". She vents that many of our schools are "little more than holding pens, releasing antsy, angry, unskilled young men into our communities".

Bloom points out that even as early as preschool, boys get expelled at five times the rate of girls because they expend more energy, have a hard time sitting still and get fidgety. They zone out until it's time for recess when they can let loose all that pent-up energy. But the problem is they also get punished and labeled early for being boisterous and disruptive by, ordinarily, a female instructor.

"The boys go home and complain that they hate school and don't want to return. Forced back each morning, they rebel and act out further, until finally the teacher has had it and they're out of there, learning their first lesson about school – their type isn't welcome there."

This phenomenon continues on through high school, widening the gap as girls take harder classes and perform better in them. More girls than boys take Advanced Placement tests and AP English, and girls "compose 64% of the National Honor Roll" in addition to collecting more school and district-wide awards. More boys drop out of high school than girls and they are prone to more risky behavior such as drinking alcohol, smoking dope, substance abuse (including prescription drugs), and joining gangs.

At this stage in history, studies are revealing that young women are proving to be far more educated than young men. One of the most prominent reasons for boys underperforming in school is that they don't READ – When asked, the attitude by many boys has been that reading is a girl thing! A multitude of test scores have shown that boys' reading proficiency is worse today than it has been in decades.

John P. Dennis

Consequently, mothers read more than fathers, and even in two-parent homes Mom is usually the one who reads their son a bedtime story. Mom takes the kids to the library and bookstores. Boys are often instructed to read by female teachers – that is one of the reasons why there is such a grand push to recruit more male teachers for primary grades. Boys love their moms, but fathers and male role models are the ones they more than likely will emulate. Seeing a man engaged in reading books can have a profound subliminal impact on them.

Poverty has a lot to do with it. Inner-city schools are often crammed with students, lacking up-to-date books and computers, begging for better educational supplies and nutritional food options, dealing with cuts to invaluable classes, filled with overstressed teachers, and more. Kids in lower economic neighborhoods have poor nutrition, constantly eat junk food and frequently go to fast food restaurants, lack motivation and drop out of school, and fall prey to drugs and gangs. Their parents hope that by entering their kids in the lottery process they might possibly luck into a good charter or magnet school. However, even under these adverse conditions girls still find a way to perform remarkably better than boys.

The greatest obstacle, or better yet - "villain", that may be causing immeasurable harm to your son and impeding his development, unbeknownst to you, is probably residing in your home ...

Your television.

Your son may not be into reading, but I'll bet he's into television. And it is something acceptable to other boys in his peer group who are not going to laugh at him as they might if they see him reading a book.

Publishers may not focus as much attention on boys as they do girls, but the media conglomerates spending billions of dollars on entertainment programming to capture and hold your son's attention certainly do! As long as it makes an enormous profit these companies could care less if these boys' motivation comes from putting their books aside and devoting most of their time to watching unmonitored YouTube videos and playing violent games on their Xboxes and iPhones, accompanied by pounding, driving beats pumping through their eardrums from iPod earbuds.

Since its inception, television has significantly influenced U.S. lifestyle, ranging from eating habits to music to fashion to consumerism to sports and politics. To be fair, over the years TV networks have broadcast shows that are inspirational, deliver pro-social messages, and positively affect viewers' lifestyle changes and children's behaviors.

Conversely, Elium and Elium declare that television stunts boys' imaginations, shortens their attention spans, and deadens their empathy for someone else's pain as a result of the violence they are exposed to.

"Television has not only affected the reading habits of our nation, but has also hindered the ability of our sons to learn to read. Their softly focused gaze as they stare at the set makes the intricate eye movements required for reading difficult and even straining on the eyes."

A comprehensive study by the University of Michigan Health System on how TV affects a child's life validates this analysis:

> *"TV can discourage and replace reading. Reading requires much more thinking than television, and we know that reading fosters young people's healthy brain development. Kids from families that have the TV on a lot spend less time reading and being read to, and are less likely to be able to read."*

Below you will discover very disturbing figures from that study on the negative traits that can be adopted from television viewing due to the widespread availability and impact of media violence on young people in America:

- *An average child will see 200,000 violent acts and 16,000 murders on TV by age 18.*

- *2/3 of all programming contains violence.*

- *Programs designed for children more often contain violence than programs designed for adults.*

- *Most violent acts go unpunished on TV and are often accompanied by humor. The consequences of human suffering and loss are rarely depicted.*

- *Many shows glamorize violence.*

- *Children imitate the violence they see on TV. Children under age eight cannot tell the difference between reality and fantasy, making them more vulnerable to learning from and adopting as reality the violence they see on TV.*

- *A 15-year-long study by University of Michigan researchers found that the link between childhood TV-violence viewing and aggressive and violent behavior persists into adulthood.*

- *A 17-year-long study found that teenaged boys who grew up watching more TV each day are more likely to commit acts of violence than those who watched less.*

- *One research study found that TV's effects on education were long-term. Watching TV as a child affected educational achievement at age 26. Watching more TV in childhood increased chances of dropping out of school and decreased chances of getting a college degree.*

Family therapist Michael Gurian views the media – specifically television, movies, and videogames – as another family member. He reasons that when a boy returns home from school and spends excessive amounts of hours watching TV unmonitored without any input from immediate family elders (i.e. mother, father, grandfather, etc) then media has to be regarded as an influential family member.

"If a parent, mentor, or educator has no opinion of the influence of the media or a very benign one – i.e., 'the media isn't something

we need to worry much about' – I would caution them. While we know the brain is forming throughout boyhood and thus any input is important, we also know from common sense that any family member has an effect on a kid, no matter the age, sex, race or interests, even if that family member is on a television screen."

On top of it all, in this digital age, studies have shown that boys ages 8-18 spend at least 7-8 hours a day on their computers, iPhones, and other electronic devices, texting, sending and receiving images, and listening to their favorite songs on their iPod; as well as spending an inordinate amount of time on social media like Facebook and Twitter. And when they do read they are usually listening to music and/or multitasking watching TV and chatting online. Boys who can barely spell spend more time texting each other than they do on their homework – because spelling doesn't matter in this context – communicating to each other is the only goal.

So how do we address this challenge? Remember, I'm a parent too, facing the same assaults on my boys. My kids were never allowed to use their shorthand when texting me. Why? Because they need to know how to communicate with respect and in the right context when dealing with figures in authority. It also allowed me to keep them in the right frame of mind...I'm not your friend, I'm your Dad. I could also monitor their command of the English language and see where they were in their writing and communication skills. Otherwise how will you see if they can write and clearly express themselves?

And beyond TV a young man's music is like an appendage to him. My concern is that we are leaving boys to their own devices and letting them discern what is good and bad without any real guidance and monitoring of what they are doing, and the type of information that is being drummed into their heads.

It's important to transfer our own values to our children. I had conversations with my sons about the messages and themes within music. To be transparent, I certainly listened to NWA and other explicit artists growing up and it didn't destroy me; yet my Mom was clear about what is acceptable and so I was able to get a standard of right or wrong from which to identify things.

So when I heard certain things in their music it was entertaining but never something I would say...it was kinda like watching a freak show since we didn't grow up in seriously violent areas. Most of it was just a little teen exploration and sampling. We hid that raunchy music from Mom, and for good reason...that was not a conversation you would want to have. Know that our sons try things without us knowing, yet, if you can get those values instilled in them then there will be something deep inside that pulls them back towards right.

Many of us are guilty about utilizing the TV as a babysitter when the kids were young because they would plop down in front of it and become mesmerized, allowing us time to take a breath or get things done around the house. I certainly did it, but made some efforts to put them in front of TV shows that coincided with our values by purchasing DVDs such as Veggie Tales (Christian cartoons) or age-appropriate movies. Small efforts here and there imparted the family values along the way. Along with all the input they get from the media, inject shows that carry messages you approve of. I found my boys were okay with watching shows that carried our values. If the TV does some "babysitting" for you then be deliberate about what it gets to convey. Little boys will watch the same show over and over, so if you have a DVD player and a little bit of effort you can put acceptable shows in front of them and they will keep them there for quite a while. On a practical level, if your boy has a TV in his room then only put a DVD player on it and not cable/satellite so you don't have any concerns about what they are watching. While they are little that will work just fine.

The overworked, stressed-out single mothers who are worried about the bills and trying to run things smoothly and hoping their son will get what he needs from school, don't have the time to monitor every show; therefore make sure to set it up so it can't get too out of control. Many single mothers and parents are oblivious to the nonstop messages and values boys are receiving from television, music, and social media; nor are they aware of how these messages are being regurgitated back out into the public. As Gurian said, we've allowed these electronic devices to become another family member.

And this "family member" is not pushing them to read.

This hypothetical scenario revolving around uncensored music posed by Lisa Bloom is something for single parents to really give thought to:

"If a violent criminal knocked on your front door and said he'd like some time alone with your son to sing some catchy and slickly packaged songs he'd written about life on the streets and behind bars, would you give him ten bucks, show him to your son's room, and leave the two of them alone for hours, unmonitored? Allowing our minor children to absorb these communications while we ignore them – and while we're even funding this stuff – is functionally the same as this scenario."

My intention is not to condemn television, digital devices, or social media. There are many positive things that can be gained from the media. Nevertheless, we can't give room to the media to be that additional "family member" who inundates our sons with unmonitored information, and then be "shocked" when they get into trouble later in life. You've seen the statistics and how boys are spending less time reading and too much time with media.

They are reading things on Social Media and watching YouTube videos you have never heard of. Even if your kid is the good kid, his friends (good and bad) will be sending him clips that could be innocent or completely foul. We all have friends that send us that foul email or picture or YouTube clip. Your son has the same thing happening to him as well. Show him that it happens with you and let him see you deal with it.

Make a concerted effort to know what your boys are watching on TV and be around to talk about unacceptable programming. Listen to music with them and talk with them about the lyrics. Discuss the violence, sexuality, etc. that the media continually broadcasts, and, as I keep reiterating, find good male role models who can discuss the more sensitive male-oriented topics with them that you and your son may be uncomfortable discussing.

"It's not macho to read? Nonsense. Reading is a stouthearted activity, disporting courage, keenness, stick-to-itness. It is also, in my experience, one of the most thrilling and enduring delights of life, equal to a home run, a slamdunk, or breaking the four minute mile."
Irving Stone

The bottom-line? Less media, more emphasis on reading for your son. Turn your house into a library if necessary, filled with as many books as you can obtain. Go to the library and go to the bookstore with him and convince his dad and/or a good male role model to do the same thing with him. Turn the TV off and read books to him and in front of him. The objective is for him to discover the pleasure of reading, and learn that it's not just to do homework.

Without developing strong reading, writing, and communication skills your son will have a tough time getting into college and being employed in today's market. There is a direct correlation between not knowing how to read and the high risks of going to prison. "The Begin to Read" program cites these statistics:

- *2/3 of students who cannot read proficiently by the end of the 4th grade will end up in jail or on welfare.*

- *85% of all juveniles who interface with the juvenile court system are functionally illiterate.*

- *More than 60% of all prison inmates are functionally illiterate.*

When all is said and done – you are the expert on your own child, and every kid is their own unique person – I can give you info, advice, etc. and then it's up to you to utilize your instincts and info, and arm yourself to go work your son into reading shape; and with this mindset I'm confident we can beat the odds!

At the end of the day he has internal and external pressures to deal with. Externally the media, social media, and peer pressures will be trying to contribute to shaping your son. Internally he will be wrestling with questions about right and wrong, relationships and manhood. Let's tackle some of those together and see if we can hit two birds with one stone!

I can remember one of my older brother's friends asking me if I had become a man yet. What he was really asking is whether I was still a virgin or not. The message conveyed though is that having sex is one of the rites of passage into manhood. It is somewhat true since you are certainly participating in an adult-level experience, but usually it's being done without the resources to deal with an unplanned pregnancy, a committed relationship, and rearing a child. Help your sons gain a healthy definition of manhood compared to adulthood. Don't let the only voice on the subject be his teen friends.

When I worked on it with my sons it was easier to impart by helping them understand that age will bring them to adulthood right on schedule. Developing into manhood means being able to take care of yourself, which includes finances, housing, food and clothing. Manhood is not based upon age. After you learn how to care for yourself then mature manhood is being able to care for any other responsibilities you bring in. Recognizing that you have to care for the needs of a child is a powerful motivator. Partner that with your faith and moral values and you should have a strong combatant against peer pressures. Let him know what it costs to have a child, from the hospital to childcare. He shouldn't feel you will rescue him, although, you know you'll help out. Help keep the pressure on. Too many guys make babies and are able to disappear back into their households. If you want to engage in adult pleasures then expect adult-level responsibilities.

Peer pressures are very real so be selective with who your child can spend time with and select as friends. Tell him specifically who you approve of and disapprove of, and why. This was a tough pill for me to swallow from my Mom growing up yet ultimately it kept me from being around a few of my neighbors who ended up in shootouts, including one who died from it. Years later I understood why Mom had set those boundaries. Thanks Mom! Expect to hear the same thing from your son because I guarantee he will see the light. Don't worry about seeming like the bad guy...for now he needs parental guidance to overshadow peer pressure.

His buddies aren't the only issue out there. Girlfriends throw their lot into the peer pressure game as well. What age should he be allowed to date? There probably isn't a set answer. If you allow it (and it may happen in secret anyway) be sure to objectively express what a good girl is and is not. Tell him a few stories about the realities of premarital sex and get that male mentor to talk over relationship issues with him as well. Staying involved as much as possible is the key. Explain to him about heartbreak and how to handle it. Lots of teen guys turn to shallow relationships because that first love hurt them pretty good. And for goodness sake don't let him date an older girl. She'll only want to show him what she has already learned.

My boys are handsome young fellas, so when an older girl wanted to move in on one of my sons the alarms went off. I explained it to him this way. "If she is such a good catch then why haven't the guys in her grade scooped her up already? She's pretty and fine so what's wrong with her? Chances are they have already dealt with her and the only guys she can catch are younger guys that don't know her." Is that true for all girls? Of course not. Do I care? Of course not! Advise your son in ways that make him wise and able to identify the red flags that we always get. My son surprised me. He agreed with my logic, but really, it shouldn't have surprised me that much. Our kids generally have a mentality fairly close to our own so they can usually accept a reasonable analysis of a situation.

Remember that you have the advantage against all these pressures because your son loves you! He wants to know what is right and acceptable. Lead the way, provide him with a roadmap through male role models/ mentors and be deliberate. Explain to him your successes and missteps along the way so that he learns how to analyze situations himself.

One of my deliberate methods is to get my son to talk it out...not give him the answer...but leave the conversation by saying, "choose wisely". As he gets older it's more important that he makes good choices, so let him practice it with good counsel. You will get back what you have invested in him. Obviously you can't let him choose in some situations but there are many that you can let him work through. Most things aren't emergencies so you can work on an issue for years to get him squared away. Don't panic. The mom that is raising her son is by far the greatest influence on his life. You are in the best position to overcome these challenges.

Chapter Seven

The Most Important Things He Needs To Learn (The Conclusion)

"I think that even though my father wasn't there, in his death and in his memory, he has been a mentor to me in my manhood because my mom couldn't teach me how to be a man.

Francis Capra

There are a lot of good quality men out there in our culture and society. Along with them there are mentoring organizations that exist to help our cause. I was mentored by senior military members, pastors and lay leaders, and online resources such as those used by John Maxwell and close friends.

Though all these tools were available, one thing I noticed as I mentored others was that it was a little bit of a crapshoot. I noticed this from those who mentored me as well. The real question that kept coming up is, "What do you talk about with this youngster?" Most guys were using their past experiences or career path development as the basis. Those within the church organizations might cover the morals and values that young men need. Yet, when mentored, along with others, we all just winged it. Based on my experiences, I wanted to put down in writing some solid precepts that need to be addressed with any young man along the way during those years of development.

Let's go over it again. Can a woman raise a boy to be a man?

No matter what the statistics show...nor what I discuss with you in this book...especially in these days and times in which single parenting is rapidly on its way to becoming the norm... people will always debate this topic – and sometimes as a point of contention.

A mother can teach her son how to be courteous to other people, to demonstrate good manners, to be a good upstanding person, and to be humble and sensitive...but she can't teach him how to be a man because she is simply not one. I recognize my redundancy on this issue, and it seems so obvious, but I'm asking you to bear with me a little longer.

It is difficult, painful, and sometimes terrifying for single mothers, as well as mothers in general (fathers too), to undergo the process of separating from their sons to allow them the natural transition to manhood. It creates an enormous amount of separation anxiety among moms, which may lead to sadness and depression as they watch their boys grow up and move away from the confines of their loving, and in some instances "restrictive", arms. But I do empathize, because in today's society, which is composed of a large number of single-parent families, the more natural rites of passage of a boy taking his steps from boyhood to manhood are not clearly defined and not as smooth. In many cases these rites are shoved aside because of fatherless homes.

Boys are taught to be men; they are not born that way. Since the beginning of time, a father's responsibility has been to raise a boy in his image, to mold and shape him, to teach him survival skills, and ultimately to instruct him on how to become a strong and responsible man. In the twenty-first century, with the advent of the huge proliferation of single mothers, it seems men are increasingly more confused about their roles as fathers, and, ironically (a fact that can't be ignored), are handicapped by the lack of training they've received to be fathers after being raised in single-mother homes themselves. Plus, they are often confronted with hostility and blame directed towards them as single dads.

There are numerous things a father figure can and should teach a boy. And when I say father figure I am including stepfathers, uncles, and mentors. Boys are more likely to model the behavior of their own father so being a role model for his son should be a father's top priority. Dad is the one from whom they learn the most about what being a man is all about. A boy watches and studies the actions and reactions, in all types of situations, of the man they are most prominently in contact with.

If there is a lack of a strong male role model in his life, a boy will spend more time bonding with media stars – sports figures, musicians, actors, etc. – and this is not necessarily a bad thing, but if those media heroes run afoul of the law, or get involved in controversial behavior, it's great to have a father figure around to help the boy interpret what he's hearing and seeing, and to explain the consequences that could result from it. You don't want him thinking, 'one day I'll defy authority, too, because I want to be just like my favorite actor'.

The right male role model can open him up to not only the right attitudes and actions, but also various ways to overcome peer, school or work pressures and development of academic interests and personal faith in God. By the way, if you want your son to have a relationship with God, expose him to men who do the same so he can see himself in that light. If he thinks this is only something the women do then he'll leave it up to the women. Steering him in the right direction starts early.

I wrote this book to help you and to help young boys face their personal struggles as I did. I hope it helps you by: 1) Sharing with you some of the battles MRWs have gone through because they lack masculine development in some areas. 2) Encouraging you to connect your son with a male that can provide healthy mentoring. 3) Providing Moms, Dads and Mentors real subjects to help get young men to a state of well-rounded development. Work on these concepts, provide a copy of this book to his mentor for reference, and be available to ensure some deliberate development. I'll move through these quickly but you should move through them slowly and adapt them to your specific needs.

Here are the essential qualities and character strengths boys need to learn and develop from you, good fathers and mentors, on their road to manhood:

RESPECT: This is one of the most important qualities and it encompasses respect in all its various forms – self-respect (if it doesn't occur within the person FIRST, then everything that follows can be negated); respect for others – men, girls and women, children, and peers; respect for authority (including parents, law enforcement, educators, and employers); respect for property; and respect for different points of view.

So how do we grow self-respect? You can Google a lot of ideas. Most of it is simple but takes a real effort. On this subject one of your main priorities should be how you talk to your son. Avoid humiliating him as a disciplinary tactic. I would always whisper to my boys in public and let them know that when they got home they could expect some "correction". It's a simple tactic and I learned it from some of my military supervisors. "Praise in Public and Counsel in Private," was the philosophy that allowed you to address an issue without embarrassing or humiliating the individual. I saw the difference when I used it with my boys. Be sure to tell them, "I'm not going to embarrass you in front of your friends because I don't want them laughing at you. I will take care of this when we get home though." Other important aspects of self-respect are grooming standards and hygiene. Teach him how to take care of himself and show him you love the person that he is. All the virtues I've included here could be their own separate books, so I'll be brief. As you read up on these character traits you'll find nifty ways to train them.

It matters on multiple levels. A secure young man cares enough about himself not to lose control or try to use intimidation tactics to gain respect. He respects himself and others on a basic level and even when those in authority behave unworthy of respect he still gives it to them by respecting their position of authority. Leaders, supervisors and managers are not always right and do not always behave admirably, but that is no excuse to dismiss their authority.

Self-respect is closely followed by respect for authority. Stay the head-of-the-house. Don't assume quickly that teachers, other parents or even officers are harassing your child when you know your child is disruptive, despite his claims to the contrary. Supporting him doesn't mean endorsing bad behavior. Even if authority is in the wrong, his best bet is to behave respectfully and then report it to you. Although I do believe we have a societal problem with some police officers, this important character trait of respect might have saved the lives of a few young men dealing with officers in the recent headlines. If it comes down to challenging authority you will always have to show where your behavior was above reproach, and that you used the proper channels to resolve the issues. That's a lesson well worth learning.

Respect for others falls in the same line. The Golden Rule is the right way to handle this. "Do unto others as you would have them do unto you." Kindness, compassion, and giving second chances are all priorities when trying to work on this one. Traits such as forgiveness and empathy will complete your young son so that he can maintain a healthy emotional state as he becomes an adult. If he sees forgiveness and empathy in you then he's likely to have the same type of disposition.

Then there is respect for other people's property. It starts with: don't touch what is not yours; pay for something if you break it; ask permission to borrow something; return something you borrow in good condition. Don't rescue your son too quickly on this one. If he breaks a window let him work it off with his allowance or by doing chores. He'll be better off having repaired or reimbursed someone for damage he's caused. That demonstrates "real" character!

MANNERS: We've all heard the expressions, "Mind your manners" or "Mind your P's and Q's", at one time or another, which is usually just a parent admonishing a child to be careful of their behavior and what they are saying. Manners are the first cousins of respect. The etiquette guru, Emily Post once commented: "Manners are a sensitive awareness of the feelings of others."

Politeness seems to be a lost art among youth today. I started my sons off with simple directives such as answering with "yes sir" and "no sir." Do they always answer this way to me? Not really, but anytime we get into a serious conversation they immediately snap to "yes sir" because they know the tone has changed. It's a minor adjustment that pays off huge dividends. Young people, particularly boys, are too busy staring at their digital devices or ensconced with the music emanating from their headphones to exhibit such polite behaviors as looking you in the eye when speaking or turning down the music to acknowledge what you have to say. Please/thank you/no thank you/yes sir, are so infrequent in a young man's jargon today that when you hear it you are genuinely surprised – you might even find yourself telling someone, "I met the nicest young man today" simply because he exhibited politeness.

It shouldn't be such a big deal, but today's narcissistic young men are wrapped up in their electronic world and forget there's a *real* world out there. Male adolescents are the guiltiest of not being mannerly because they'd prefer to showcase their coolness and swagger in place of polite behavior, accompanied by expectations of respect they haven't rightfully earned. They need to be taught that polite behavior, good manners, communicating and learning how to speak up, and not being too cool to smile, are good habits to learn, and constitute a way of life that can take them to far greater heights.

INTEGRITY: This was a hard one to get my kids to see. I would always explain to my boys to tell the truth about what happened...even if it

John P. Dennis

means they might get into trouble. "The cover-up is worse than the crime." Everyone makes mistakes, but when you lie about it you compound the issue. But integrity really isn't just about lying...it's about being true to your values even when your actions are hidden. It's what you do when no one is looking but you and God. Help your little boy see that you expect his behavior to be the same whether you are present or not. That was the type of trouble I had with my adopted daughter. Around me she was an angel; but away from me she was a completely different character. Eventually that double life caught up with her, and now no one feels they can trust her to behave. If they don't practice your values when they are away from you then you still have more work to do, because they are picking up ideals from elsewhere.

The media is the worst purveyor of integrity and trustworthiness. Reality television shows make a fortune featuring celebrities who are dishonest, unfaithful, devoid of integrity, and willing to do anything to win a contest or "get over" on a perceived opponent. Usually the message conveyed in these shows is – do whatever you have to do, and by any means necessary – to not just succeed, but conquer – no matter who gets hurt in the process. Boys and young men have to be weaned from the TV in order to be taught virtues such as integrity and trust, and to understand that it is a process and not something inherited or gained overnight. It's all about learning how to make the right choices, and being honest and accountable for what you did – right or wrong.

SELF-DISCIPLINE: Self- discipline is another way of saying self-control. So don't advocate him losing control. This starts as early as the little fits or tirades that 2-year-olds test out on us. My boys did it too and found out that it was a pretty bad idea to throw an anger fit in Walmart over the toy he wanted. After a little correction we made sure they understood that if they wanted something they simply asked for it. If we said no then we had a reason: sometimes you don't deserve it...it's too expensive for my budget...it's not for your age, or maybe I just wanted to get it for your birthday or Christmas instead of right now; but that little fit means you need to learn other lessons first.

Learning how to manage your emotions when you're feeling crazed because of something unexpected occurring outside of your control is at the heart of self-discipline. These kinds of lessons have an impact on your whole life. Adolescents have to understand that the wrong reaction can place their lives in jeopardy – including the lives of friends or family who may be with them. When you're accidentally rear-ended by a car and your son erupts in anger instead of coolly assessing the situation, it may result in an unnecessary road rage situation causing people to get hurt or possibly killed...it's too late for self-discipline at that point!

Even worse, if he is wrongly stopped by the police and, instead of reigning in his pride, no matter how justified he is, he chooses to speak belligerently to the officers questioning him, he will have unwittingly aggravated the situation because he hasn't learned how to talk to authority figures.

Encourage your son to get involved in sports, music, and other activities that involve daily routines and practice, teamwork, and self-sacrifice...traits that can enhance and develop a boy's character, which he will carry with him throughout his lifetime. Participating in extra-curricular activities will give you a chance to teach him not to quit when things are tough, and how to practice and improve himself. These attributes are big commodities in the real world and will help secure his self-image, knowing he can accomplish things he sets his mind to.

RESPONSIBILITY: Ever since Adam and Eve, men have been ducking responsibility, trying to tie blame to anyone but themselves. It's a sad sad state when usually all that is required is to say, "That was my fault," but you can't even fess up to it. It's because I didn't have a Dad...we were poor..."the Man" is keeping me down...they start out with an advantage over me...and on and on. This is a hard concept for many to swallow so I will try to relay it slowly – LIFE IS NOT FAIR. I can't make it fair and neither can you...but what does that really mean? Basically it boils down to the fact that some people have an advantage in life and some people are disadvantaged. It could be financially, musically or genetically. Some have influential political figures in their family and others are descended from long lineages of wealth and privilege. You get to choose whether that is good or bad news. Simply put, it means you can work to achieve all your own goals in life and pass on an advantage to your own family.

Think about that.

It's not about what you don't have...what you DO have is enough to get started, but you have got to stop making excuses for reasons not to succeed. Fear of Failure is often cited as a reason, so many give up or don't even try. I'd wager Fear of Success paralyzes more people than Fear of Failure. I've seen young men who just don't want the responsibility of supervising, and definitely not managing. So is it someone else's fault that you were not promoted?

But this is about what boys need to learn.

Don't let him get away with blaming others for the trouble he gets into, because moms can be very protective of their sons. For example, you know he can be a terror and full of energy. When the teacher tells you he was disruptive in class don't go searching for what the other kids were doing. He needs to learn that merely associating with misconduct, even if he is not involved, can implicate him. It's a priceless skill to be able to avoid trouble, because no matter what you are doing, sometimes your presence alone can get you deemed an "accessory" by the law. You can point fingers all you want, but ultimately simple principles provide the best solutions. Teach him not to let his name be associated with troublemakers or trouble in general...no excuses. He is responsible for his own conduct.

TRUSTWORTHINESS: To be worthy of trust what will he need to do? These different character traits build upon each other. The values of being honest and responsible build the foundation of trustworthiness. Give him small responsibilities – from cleaning his room to taking out the small can of trash from the restroom – and start to practice them. Use daily tasks, then let him practice doing them without being told. In short...build trust. Teach him to be true to his word. In time you move him up into higher and higher responsibilities, while explaining to him that as he shows he can handle greater responsibilities it opens up greater liberties and privileges for him. You don't have to lock him away to keep him safe. You have to help instill inner principles that allow him to navigate life and avoid trouble along the way.

FAIRNESS: While the world is not fair, employers are not fair, and teams and everything else seem to be unfair, the simple fact remains that your young man needs to be taught fairness. It starts as simple as playing by the rules. If he steps on the line then he is out of bounds...don't cheat. Cheating can become a part of your character. You win some and you lose some but a win while cheating is actually a loss. Sooner or later taking the shortcut will cost you the price of the entire journey, or more. He doesn't need to see you cheating and you don't need to cheer him on if he cheats. Winning at the cost of your character is too high a price.

CARING: We share this planet with each other so let's do some things to help each other. When my sons donated time to help clean homes after flooding in Missouri I got to see firsthand the kind of hearts they were developing. Helping others actually helps you, so give your son some exposure and participation with charities. Seeing and aiding others less fortunate than yourself is a good way to learn gratitude for what your Mom has done for you. Encourage "caring" instead of toughness and you'll find that he can be tough and caring at the same time.

Most people end up needing to dish out a little "tough love" at some point, and in truth it's driven by a caring heart that is willing to make the difficult decisions. When he gets to see that life can be very hard he will grow to understand why you gave him certain restrictions to try and keep him on track. That was your way of caring for him.

CITIZENSHIP: My first effort in the area of citizenship came as a Cub Scout picking up litter along the roadway in front of our church. I still remember it to this day and because of it you couldn't get me to sling trash out of a window if you tried. By the time I was a young adult I had volunteered with the Special Olympics, nursing home visits, Dept. of

Corrections, work release centers and Big Brother programs, just to name a few. Those small efforts made me a better person, and my community a better place to live. This extends all the way to voting and being an active member of our communities. You'll get to see the difference Teacher/Parent programs make when you visit a school without one. Each singular effort adds up when we all play a part, and it starts with something as small as picking up trash in your yard (and maybe your neighbor's yard). When it snowed in St. Louis and my boys shoveled the sidewalks I'd have them shovel our elderly neighbor's portion as well.

Look for those opportunities...

Well that's it, but before you're done take a look at the startling and candid interviews some of the men gave for this book. I also added some of the troubling statistics so you can see just how many people are in this struggle with you. It's already tough so you don't need me to restate the obvious. There is a way to overcome all these obstacles.

I promised you some good news though and the good news is that these principles work. If you want to grow an apple tree then plant an apple seed. Each of these character traits can be planted in the soft soil of a young child and like an expectant farmer you can watch and wait to see your effort bear fruit. Down at the core your young man will lean on these guiding principles to make choices, manage relationships and avoid trouble. It was easy for me to skirt around trouble because my character disagreed with rowdy conduct. There was an internal compass that steered me away from people and problems that came my way. At the same time this compass steered me towards men that were good role models. Instead of seeing the "nerd" that never partied, I noticed guys that were getting their education, promotions and taking care of their families. I wanted to be like that more than I wanted to be cool and that is exactly what I became. Individuals that were wiser than me planted these seedlings in me and they continue to sprout up. This is not a guess or an experiment! I am telling you what I know to be true! This is a testimonial and I know you love your son because I know my Mom loves me. If you've been asking and praying for help then found some here. Trust me. It worked for me...it worked for my three sons and it will work for you.

Dad if you are reading this I hope it helps you know what your son might be going through or maybe even addresses things that you went through yourself. Your son needs you to show him how to be a man. If you worry that you aren't that good at it then used the principles as a guide. It will work for you. Financial support is not the greatest thing you can do for your son. Giving him your wisdom and insight will bless him much greater and give you a rich relationship you will treasure for life. I tried to work win over Mom so she would value your input as well so maybe this can be a jumpstart for you. Perhaps you could buy the book for the mother of your son to get things started. No matter how you do it I believe you can impact your son's life.

Then to all those men that are out there mentoring young boys and men that are not your own I pass along a sincere THANK YOU. You are changing lives and I know your effort makes a difference.

God Bless You! We can do it together!

APPENDIX 1:

TRANSCRIPTS OF INTERVIEWS

RESPONDENT #1 (Pastor/MFT Intern)

I first became aware of being raised by a single mother around when I was about 10. The reason is, I played piano for around 5 years, I loved to play, didn't like to practice, and my mother and I would fight every night about me practicing. It was the first time I had ever felt I didn't have someone on my side, an absence, an unfair advantage, me against my mother, and no one on my side. I felt like I wasn't being heard and it was because I was a kid. I'd see other kids interacting and I'd notice a father say in the kid's defense to his mother...okay, slow down. I realized I didn't have that in my relationship with my mother.

And then when puberty hit I didn't know what in the world was going on. I knew I couldn't go to her about it.

When I was a kid around 8 or 9 I asked my mother 'where's my dad'? (*His father tragically died when he was an infant.*) My mother told me he got sick and died, not the specifics. In fifth grade I remember going to my teacher after we had gotten back from summer vacation and all the boys were talking about what they did with their dad and it really hurt me that I didn't have that experience for summer. At lunchtime I asked her, "Do you think it's fair that all the boys talk about what they did with their dads and I don't have a dad?" And she said, "I understand what you're saying, but if you had a dad and there were things you guys did during the summer, wouldn't you talk about him, too?" And I agreed. It was one of the first times I was aware that there was supposed to be another parent in my life and there was not. I remember thinking, since I don't have a dad...God was going to be my dad. And that was the first time I thought about a relationship with God because God was filling in for the father I didn't have. I was in a church school and I figured the father figure I was going to have was this one.

Sometimes kids asked me about my dad and I gave them the same answer as my mother told me, he got sick and died. And they'd ask me how and I'd say I didn't really know.

How were you disciplined?

Arguing and yelling, and now and then a spanking – maybe three times in my life and I got it. Basically yelling at me. Mom made it very clear very early that you don't talk back, don't sass me.

I remember my mother (around age 8-11) exclusively dating a man...but if she picked me up from school and had a bad day at work – she talked to me about it. And if she cried about it, she cried to me about it. It was a lot emotional responsibility that I received from her. She would pour her heart out to me so that she wouldn't have to with him. I just had to sit there and listen. She complained to me about family. She came to me with her adult problems and I didn't know what to do with it. I was a smart nerdy kid and sometimes mature, but when I would act my age my mother would sometimes come to me and say, I don't know how to deal with you when you act your age...because to her I was always acting older.

John P. Dennis

Did you feel pressure to be the man of the house?

Oh yeah…and my mother didn't understand it. I tried to talk to her a few years ago and it just went over her head. Very early on I felt responsible for her, especially emotionally, because I knew financially I couldn't do anything for her. For example, I'll never forget when I was a teenager, my mother had a terrible day at work. The man she was seeing had a key to the house and opened the door and I immediately went over to him and whispered to him as he walked inside, "Mom's had a terrible day, so you might want to take it easy on her." He thanked me for letting him know. A lot of her emotional stress I took on for myself. But what's interesting is, I kind of rebelled against her by not cleaning my room because I knew she was a "neat freak" and I knew she would get upset. That was my passive-aggressive way of getting back at her.

Back to puberty and your voice changing, etc. - how did you feel with your mom? What did you do about it – did you have anyone to go to?

That was a horrible time…I didn't go to anybody. My mother and I didn't have the TALK. When I was 8 years old she gave me a book called "Where DID I COME FROM?" that was really well illustrated and said 'read this' and that was it! That was our conversation…so when I was becoming a man and going through those physical changes of becoming a young man…I didn't know whom to talk to about it. She wouldn't even let me talk to my uncles about it…she felt like all the men in our family had trouble with women… she felt all her brothers were abusers so that was the last thing she wanted me to know anything about and didn't want me to pick up those habits of womanizing or possibly being abusers. But their relationships with women had nothing to do with their physical developments as men.

The other part is, I grew up with epilepsy so for me I learned just in living that I noticeably had drawn a correlation that when I went to any extreme I had a seizure, so if I were extremely happy or sad or tired or any extreme…I had a seizure. So my thought was then, I can't orgasm because it might end up in a seizure and I would scare everyone. So for years that's how I thought…and knowing how people responded when they saw the seizure and how panicked they got, I didn't want to put anybody else through that...so to me it was: I better not do this thing...

I had sex for the first time when I was 19 and still had that very much on my mind and actually trained myself not to ejaculate or orgasm because of this fear. But what I learned from talking to women is that some women feel they didn't please you if you didn't orgasm. So I lost a girlfriend in those early days due to not having an orgasm with her.

How did you learn about sex?

My best friend's mother and stepfather were married and they were very much in love and touchy-feely, so I watched and studied them...but I never had a source of info about this...I'd see movies and hear what the guys would say, but I knew half of them were making stuff up and lying in high school...I never got the sit-down conversation with anyone or learned much, so I had to learn as I grew as an adult – books, conversations, talking to women - because I never had that.

What vibe did you get from your mother about meeting women, intimacy, and parties?

It was difficult with my mother...even as a grown adult when I got back from the seminary. She eventually got married and did what they do in their bedroom...when I would go out and come home late, she'd have the light on and question me about what I did that night...grill me! And even if I was leaving to go out on a date or whatever...she would state the ultimate buzzkill before I left – 'well, don't forget about Aids!' She went there every time with stuff like this. It was not pleasant...

Elaborate on how she grilled you...what types of questions?

She'd sit up with the light on and ask me as soon as I walked in the door: "It's 2:00, it's 3:00 in the morning, why didn't you call me?" I'd answer, "I'm a grown man." Her response was, "but you're in my house!"

The first time I had sex was in a car down the hill from our house...I came in and my clothes were messed up...she looked at me and asked repeatedly, "What did you do?" She had a full-length mirror and took me over there and my clothes were all jacked up and she'd ask, "Did you have sex?" "Yes." "Did you wear a condom?" "No." And then it was like, forget about it – it led to a 2-hour lecture – you could have Aids, etc.

My mother was extremely overprotective (much of it probably due to being widowed when I was an infant and my problems with epilepsy). Honestly I think there was a part of her that never wanted me to have anyone else in my life that might surpass her – I really think that. So, me dating and having sex meant that might be a possibility and she didn't want that. I was an adult when she remarried and even then it was strange...it was weird...and they were in the room having sex and doing what they wanted to do, she would still be the same way with me...she did the same thing... he tried to back her off...but she'd talk to me later and say her husband thought that she pushed too hard...but then she'd remark, "I'm sorry, but, you know why I did that, right?"

She met a few of the women I dated when I was living at home and she has not met any since. She was always nice to them, but when I got home... I'd get a grilling – I don't like her...she's too fat, she's too slow...there was always something wrong with the women I brought home. I had never dated a woman and heard my mother say, "I really like her." She was great at putting up a great front. But as soon as they went home then you'd hear how my mother really felt about them.

Do you feel you missed not having a male presence in your life?

Oh yeah...I missed a male presence in my life. First of all, even growing up with the epilepsy...I still liked sports, like basketball, etc. I think if I'd had a father figure in the house, I probably would have gotten to play on a team in high school because he would have said – aw let him play. I remember my urologist and he'd ask, 'Why didn't you ever play sports?' and I'd tell him because of the seizures, and he'd say high school coaches are trained for stuff like that...they know when to put you in and take you out. That was one of the things...the other is...I had resentment later in my life, like when I mentioned that during the time I was 10, I didn't feel I had anyone on my side...that my mother would argue, and I didn't have a voice or anyone on my side...so I felt shut down. I think a father or father figure would have, at least I would have hoped, explained to me what she was trying to say, meant, or what she was trying to explain to me. Or stand up for me at times. It meant something to me later in life when my stepfather went to bat for me.

In my late twenties I remember my uncle and stepfather, and my aunt that I didn't know very well had just died and I wanted to go to the funeral in Oklahoma. My mother just out of the blue said, "Why do you want to go to that funeral? You didn't know her? And both my uncle and stepfather went – 'oh my goodness!' I went to my room and I guess both of them gave her a tongue lashing...she came to me later and said 'they both said I was wrong for saying that, but you knew what I meant' and explained herself again. I ended up still not going to the funeral. It was one of those times I had father figures in my house and they both stood up for me.

The only organized ball I played was at the Y during fourth or fifth grade, and even though I was the worst player on the team – I loved it. I was hoping to play some kind of organized ball and my natural inclination since my uncle and cousin had played ball was for me to do so too. The problem was my mother blocked and would not let me try out anything... her reasoning and rationale was that I would have a seizure and just be a mess...I remember the P. E. teacher and football coach trying to encourage me to come try out. I didn't even bother to mention it to my mother because she had already turned me down on basketball...football was even worse. After therapy I understand it better now, but because I felt so emotionally responsible for my mother I didn't want to do anything that would upset her. I knew trying out for sports, despite what she said, would upset her, so I didn't push the issue. I could have played baseball, less contact...but still she didn't want me to play anything for fear of the seizure.

Hypothetically, even if I hadn't had seizures, knowing her, I think she still would have come up with another reason for not allowing me to play. What might have been different is that I might have gone ahead anyway, because I would have had more self-confidence.

Talk about the level of independence in your daily life.

I didn't get involved in any other activities in school. My life was - go to school, go home, study...that's been the pattern most of my life. It wasn't until I went to seminary that I realized I could have a life...but even in the back of my mind I still limited myself. I went to counseling in the seminary and my mother hated the idea of counseling. She feared I was going to talk about her all the time...in part she was right. I was physically independent being elsewhere in college, but not emotionally...and I would still tell her things... she would call me the exact times every week after my counseling sessions and grill me about 'what did you talk about'... 'I know you talked about me for 1-2 hours of this'. It was torture and she'd cry and say 'you talked about me and I did the best I could...why are you even going to that person?' To this day she still talks about it...constant grilling...it does something to a person...it really hurt me...I couldn't even see a therapist without her putting up an objection. Even now the therapist I've been seeing since I was 25, my mother asks me literally 'what's her name' and 'where's her office and phone number'. I'd tell her, 'Mom, this is private...I'm not going to tell you', and to this day she still asks me. She feels entitled to everything in my life...she can have a life outside of me, but not me outside of her. When my stepfather and uncle died it became my responsibility to take care of her. I have had the thought there are times when I think my mother only had me so she would have someone to take care of her...I know it's not true, but it feels that way. I see other mothers with children and I don't see this level of control and emotional dependency.

We've talked about me not being married and me not being in a relationship and my mother's words of wisdom to me were, "Well don't worry about it, it's not all it's cracked up to be – you have to worry about other people when you're married and you have to worry about her – enjoy your freedom."

Do you think losing her husband and your father so early in life has something to do with it?

Yes...and her father was not a very nice person...so from grandpa she got a distrust of men. It was reinforced by my dad because he would go on weekend benders and they wouldn't see each other from Friday night to Monday morning...and he worked hard from Monday-Friday...but he wasn't a real source of strength and me being an only child and sickly, led her to pour everything into me.

When I was growing up and interested in girls my mother would tell me, I'm a woman too...so when you bring those girls some flowers, you bring me home some too...and I'd think, really? I'm not dating you...I'm dating her.

Summary/advice

No matter how close you are to your mother you are not tied to her...the umbilical cord was cut from her when you were a baby...and every person has a right to be their own person, meaning they have to separate from their parents. It's hard, but it's okay and healthy – you won't love your mom any less and you have to love yourself too.

What would you say to a single mother about raising a son?

Learn the difference between protecting him and emasculating him. A boy has to learn how to be a man. I think my mom was right in one way – she could teach me how to treat a woman, but she couldn't teach me how to be a man. What that means is you have a responsibility for putting a man in a position he can be taught by. If the guy you find in your life is upstanding and someone you can respect, make sure that guy has a relationship with your child so that your son can learn what it is to be a man from him.

RESPONDENT #2 (Therapist/Counselor)

When did you realize your father wasn't a part of your life?

I remember them not being together...my earliest recollection was them constantly arguing. The relationship was ruptured. I remember my father shaving with one of those old shavers...lathering up...I remember standing in the bathroom watching him shaving and was fascinated by that...awed by it (I was around 5). I can vividly remember the song "Charlie Brown...he's a clown..." coming on while he was shaving. After that, my next memory was of them separating. After that point there was no relationship and I remember them not being together. The next vivid recollection was of him being gone. Never got an explanation and never asked about it. My mother was feisty. Her behavior gave me the message that he was not a good person. She seemed like she was always angry with him...she never said anything bad about him, but you got the feeling she didn't like him... free-flowing anger about him, but never said anything bad about him. But when she said I could go see him there was reluctance in her attitude – well go ahead, it's your dad. I'm still not sure what happened in the marriage that led to divorce.

What I did know about my father was that he was kind of a street man and hung out on Avalon Blvd....he would go to a bookie, to a bar, hang out in the barbershop on the same block. When I was with him we would go to the bookie and all these places and I would just hang out with him. We'd walk around, go to Wrigley Field, which was on 42nd and Avalon. Never anything regarding sports or went to a baseball game or other sporting event, or even talked about it. Never played catch, nothing like that...not one time. Divorced when I was about 5 or 7.

How often did you see your father?

No regular visits, more intermittent...spontaneous. My mother always made it an announcement, not because I was continually asking. It was more like 'you need to see your dad'...or maybe at times he asked to see me, but I really don't know. As I got older I would ask to see him because I wanted to be around him. Even so, we didn't do much beyond walking around, getting a haircut, aunt's beauty shop, bar, etc., and he would be with his friends and I was just kind of there...no planned or specific activities. I would go over to where he stayed; he had a girlfriend and we would all hang out and watch TV. Only one time I can remember going to a game at Wrigley Field and going into the stadium with him. It was close to our home where I could actually hear the noise at the stadium.

My mother never questioned me about my activities. The one thing he would do is always give me money after each visit, $10, $5, etc...that was a big thing. I can vaguely remember her asking him for money - for clothes, and essentials like that. 'They need shoes' and stuff like that she would ask for. I can remember him and his running buddy. I remember in my freshman year...him being on the periphery...when I broke my leg in football. I had a lot of promise...my father came over with his buddy to see me and I was laying on the couch and he said, "yeah you're a little too light to be playing football..." like he wasn't surprised that I got hurt. That was his assessment, no praise, that was it. I don't remember him attending any of the games I played. I found it very bizarre...no encouragement...no comfort. Never came to my games and I don't remember inviting him...no protocol...and I never asked, because he was never really around.

He died in my early twenties. When he passed, I remember being at his funeral and feeling like I SHOULD be crying, but I didn't. I felt guilty about not crying even after seeing my mother crying and everyone else. I tried to make myself cry and if I did they were forced. I was looking around seeing people wailing, and feeling awful that I wasn't doing the same thing. I mustered up some tears, but it didn't feel real...it wasn't natural and I never had that connectedness or relationship with him. Never had talks about girls, women, never had the birds and bees conversation...didn't have it with my mother, either. I kind of winged it...learned from others and grappled on my own. I'm sure there were times I pretended to know what people were talking about and I kind of fumbled my way through it, but no, none of those talks...I got info from health class, but that's as far as it went in regards to a more formal education.

Did your mother push you toward any male role models or men to speak with?

What she did is put me in the cub scouts and boy scouts...it was her way of giving us that male presence...she put us in sports – baseball, basketball, etc. I was around my Uncle Charlie. During that time she had several boyfriends, but I never established a relationship with any of them. I remember one man being a nice guy. What I do remember is whenever my mother went out, my brother and I would wait and stay up all night until my mother came home and then we would jump into the bed. We were by ourselves and my mother would occasionally check. She would come home around twelve. Sometimes she came home with someone – particularly the long-established relationship. I remember one boyfriend was very good to my mother and financially supportive. He was kind of quiet, not overly nice to us. We might go by his upholstery shop and we would wait in the car for her...maybe she was waiting to get some money or something else...this included waiting in the car when she'd go to our aunt's beauty shop and we'd have soda pop (orange and strawberry crush), sandwiches and snacks, candy, etch-a-sketch, comic books, etc. – it could be a four-hour wait...and sometimes she'd show her boys off to the ladies and we'd walk through the beauty parlor to use the bathroom and go back to the car.

Was it more noticeable you didn't have a dad around other kids?

Never felt I was missing a dad with the other kids. Never felt jealous, we were so young; it was just a part of our lives. My father's nickname was "Tump". His real first name was Travis. Before he passed, I remember going and seeing him in the hospital, I remember vaguely something wrong with his stomach...girlfriend much younger than him...never got the whole story, but I think she stabbed my dad and I remember going and seeing him and she was there taking care of him. Somehow it was alluded to that she had done it. But from that illness, he got sicker, and I don't know if this was related but I remember him being in the hospital and him having cancer and being in the bed. He had a lot of hair and I would pick his hair out and rub stuff in it...I remember a big lump in his hair and being shocked by the lump and I kept rubbing it. He ended up having cancer and I think it spread – and he passed that day and I remember a weird look he gave me when I left...it was like he was trying to establish something at that point. It also established how disconnected you can be.

My mother seemed to have an angry and frustrated demeanor...she would get mad a lot about anything and she was kind of a yeller. She could be hyper-critical and say 'you won't be doing that'. I knew she really loved us and she would do anything she could for us...but we didn't have those family talks or say 'I really love you' or things. It was a non-issue...it's hard to explain...we knew my mom loved us, but there was no coddling. My mother was an only child and I think that had something to do with it. She was always in survival mode wondering where the next check was going to come from to buy clothes and food; that was more of her concern... keeping a roof over our heads. She never said 'I don't have any money and you guys need to get out there'. I remember going out and cutting lawns on my own. That was my way of making my own money. I remember her getting paid on Fridays and those were good days when we could have fish and candy treats, etc.

I think she felt anger from her marriage with my dad and it was the type of anger where she felt she wasn't going to let anyone push her around... nobody was going to misuse or abuse her or take advantage of her... she had that kind of posture about herself. She'd get mad really quick. I remember when she got married to Louie she'd get pissed off with him all the time, complaining that he'd let people take advantage of him, and we'd tell her 'if this is his decision why are you getting mad?' She eventually got divorced and married Gus. She was married to him about 4 years. She was very controlling and some people say mad all the time...anything could pop her off. I remember her being argumentative with my dad. I'd worry about the marriage not lasting because she could be too mean. My brother and I would sometimes have to go get her because Louie would say 'come get your mother'. As a result she would sometimes think we were against her. She sometimes escalated in her anger, which made me think there were other things bothering her.

Do you know much about your mother's early upbringing?

I don't know much about my mother's upbringing...I know she came out here from Texas and got divorced shortly after she was here. She ended up going to UCLA. She broke her back when she was young. I know her father got divorced and married a much younger woman. My mother didn't talk a lot about her upbringing. My mother was close to my dad's family. There was a lot of unspoken stuff between us.

Never laid adult problems on us. She might say 'I don't have any money'... she never cried on our shoulders about a man, etc.

I remember having a hip injury when I was around 9 or 10 and I was kept at children's hospital for 3 or 4 months and they put me in a body cast up to my neck...but before they put on the cast they would do a body range, holding me down - that was very painful. It was a big disconnect and I was not with my family and my mother came to see me sometimes...not a lot... my father didn't come at all...it was inflammation of that bone. I guess what I'm trying to say is there was a gap where I was not with anybody. I saw the therapist more than I saw my family because he would come and see the kids every day.

My mother was fine with me seeing girls...it amused her when girls thought I was cute. Never talked to me about getting a girl pregnant. Once, she flipped the mattress on her Saturday cleaning and found my girlie magazines and condoms but didn't say anything, just kind of looked at me, but that was it...even after that, we never had that conversation...never had that talk with anyone.

I have no mechanical aptitude...no idea...even up to today. I make it as a joke – if you guys are depending on me, forget it, because I've never learned. My father was not around so I never had that posture about being the breadwinner...the man of the house...it could almost be to my detriment...even with my wife, I don't feel I needed to be the man or make more money...a lot of women want the guy to be that way and that's not me. My wife and I have had that conversation...it's part of my making...I've never been threatened by a strong woman...

I did feel the need to be with my father at all costs...I didn't care what people thought about him, I felt like I needed to be around him even though we didn't have this great relationship...but I just wanted to be around him. My mother was angry and under pressure. I wanted to be around him simply because he was my father...

In one of the studies I reviewed there is a propensity or a need to be with that person who rejected you. It was the first time that hit me why I wanted to be with my father all the time, even though he wasn't around and he wasn't that fatherly figure. I had a need to always take it or leave it...there was some part of me crying out 'why doesn't he call?' Why doesn't he say 'I'm coming to get you, son?' So invariably I always wanted to be with him. What did I do? Why not me? Seeing that study is the first time it put it into perspective for me. Even though I knew my mom really didn't like my dad and he was not a good man.

I was very protective of my mother. My mom was everything to us and we didn't ever want to see her hurt so we were very protective of her. That's why when she went out we were worried, and would sit by the window waiting, and it was a big relief when she showed up. There was still a level of responsibility that we felt. We had chores. She spanked us because she felt that was what she had to do raising two boys. She made sure we went to church ever since we were little. Even if she didn't go, we had to go...did not learn a lot of touching and affection...didn't show a lot of emotion except frustration...she wore how she felt. It wasn't like she was trying to be mean to us – she was emotionally driven and her emotion was frustration and anger.

She established a style, a tone for how we learned to handle things, I think my brother even more so than me...he is very critical and high-strung and that's how my mom is. My wife says I took on that person too and that I'm hyper-critical and not aware of it. I would approach people who didn't do things the way I saw it and sometimes be overly critical, just critical and not having the empathy...that's why I think I drifted into psychology...I was learning about myself on an unconscious level. People would say I'm so empathic. I also see now how much my mother sacrificed...she was under the gun a lot...sometimes I can't believe it. It was through the organizations (i.e. boy scouts, sports) that I learned my "manliness" that she put me in.

I wouldn't let anybody punk me, but I don't feel like I had to overcompensate by getting into fights. My brother took on more of my mother's personality type. He had nobody to bounce it off of – that was the model he took more of the traits from...he'd pop off faster.

Advice to a single mom

Awareness...when they think the child is not observing them or internalizing them – they are and everything you do. Be aware of how you're affecting that child. I think a single parent can raise a young man and be great, but as long as they are aware of how they affect the child. I don't think you have to have a man's perspective...or have him come into your life. I think the pivotal thing is to be aware you are affecting that child in every kind of way. The kid takes on your emotions, your sensibilities. I don't believe a mother raising a son automatically makes them more feminine or overly sensitive...I think it is a combination of environment and you.

What did happen with my brother and me is that we are more emotionally driven...and I think that does have a lot to do with my mom because she was an emotional person and less logical or intellectual about my emotions. We didn't spend time assessing but much of that emotion comes from frustration and anger and that's how we learned to handle adversity, that became our style...on that level it's more of a womanly thing...that makes more sense to me and characteristic of women. I can remember thinking with my mom 'why are you so upset?' 'Why do you have to take it to that level?' It was baffling to me. It was at the drop of a hat sometimes. My brother took on that persona about situations that didn't seem to call for it...it wasn't that serious...coming from my frame of reference it seemed like he was a frustrated angry person.

I remember getting into a thing with my mother and he'd look at me like 'you shouldn't talk to our mother like that' – he would almost immediately take her side. It was almost like he became the man of the house when I came back after being going for a long time. Here I come back, not disrespectful and he was suddenly like 'just do what she said' – and suddenly I became the rebel...it was weird and suddenly I was the bad guy...he was with my mother for three years when I was gone and he took on that defense. And I remember on a drive with the three of us to San Francisco thinking they're just alike when they got into an argument on each other's driving, <u>yet my wife thinks I'm a lot like my mother.</u>

RESPONDENT #3 (Correctional Officer)

Family Background

I'm from a single-parent home. I did have a relationship with my father, in fact a great relationship. I grew up in a small town in North Carolina; originally I was born in Yonkers, NY. We moved to NC when I was about 2 and lived with my grandmother and I've been here ever since, although I would go back and forth to NY for the summer or to visit family up there. Spent most of my life in NC. I was raised pretty much by my mother's mother and my father's mother. My father later moved back to North Carolina when we moved there. When I was growing up my father used to come by all the time. My father was very much involved in my life.

Sounds like you grew up with a lot of women in your life; did that affect you in any way?

No, it kind of evened out...my dad wasn't in the house with me, but I saw him pretty much every day and I spent a lot of time with my uncles – he has ten brothers...so I have a host of male cousins, so I had plenty of male figures to be around.

Tell me about the type of work you do.

I work in the prison...I'm in law enforcement, a corrections officer...I've been doing that for almost 11 years...started out with the Sheriff's department...a lot of the stuff I've been involved in was on the street levels, so I'd see them coming in off the streets. The Sheriff's Department is a little different from what I do now – it's more contact with the males on the street, especially the ones involved in different activities – gang activity, drugs, whatever they're doing I see them. I develop a rapport with them after dealing with them on a regular basis. Now I'm in a federal system, no longer on the street level, and actively dealing with more of them coming out of town and from different areas...less of the local ones...a broader range of people that I am dealing with.

Give me an idea what was a routine day when you were working with the Sheriff's Dept.?

My duties then were to monitor them when they were locked up, arrested, booked...when you're dealing on a local level, jail is different from a prison, they come in and out...you may have a bond, someone to come and bail you out...you could be in jail for an hour...the police may lock you up long enough for you to sober up or to come down off of whatever you're on, trespassing, fighting at the club...then you're thrown in jail and can get back out...I could process you in jail and possibly see you later on that day at Walmart...but dealing with you on a prison sentence you're going to be with me for a minute...it will be some time before I see you on the streets again.

I know statistics cite it, but based on your experience, did you find a large population of men raised by single mothers in the jail and prison population?

Yes.

Any percentages?

Jail or prison?

Give me both if possible, in your estimation.

With jail it's harder to say because of the high turnover rate, so many demographics of people...for example, the rally with Mike Brown and Eric Garner, they arrested 30 people, out of those people probably 50% come from two-parent homes, generally those people come from good homes, college students, standing up for a good cause...it's harder to put your finger on it...so the jail is much more difficult to say. But in the prison I have more of a chance to find more things about them and they have a caseload. I monitor their daily activities, do their mail, security, etc. I'm going to say 60% if not even higher come from one-parent homes. It's pretty alarming when you think about it.

How do you assess this?

Most of this comes from conversations with them, talking, visiting habits... many times when they have a visitor it's usually their mom, not their dad. Their mail usually gets scanned so when I read their letters it's ordinarily from mom, no mention of their dad...things like that you learn to watch for and pick up when you're dealing with them.

I know this can be difficult to discern, but do you notice, or rather, can you tell the difference from those prisoners that have been raised by single mothers? Are there any types of characteristics that stand out?

Most of the guys who were raised by their moms tend to be a little more compassionate towards women, depending on their relationship with their mom. If they have bad relationships with their mother, for instance they might tell me they had a terrible relationship with their mother... I've had guys tell me that they didn't get along with their mom, that she abandoned them...she may also have been a large part of their lives, but they didn't have a good relationship with her. So it reflects later on the way they treat women they come into contact with...whether it be authoritative figures like the warden, the officers, the counselor, etc...it reflects their relationship with their mom.

Do you find many have children of their own?

Yes. Quite a few have children. Some are involved with the lives of their children, some are not. A large amount are not involved...some want to be, but are not allowed...others have no interest, although there are very few that don't, at least, have an interest. What I've found is most of them don't have a good relationship with the mother.

John P. Dennis

I've reviewed a lot of statistics on the prison situation, but it's great to speak with someone like you who is there and talks to people every day.

It's hard to get a just perspective when you're not actually there...it's just like anything else, it's hard for me to know what's really going on in the neighborhood or streets if I'm disconnected and I don't have intel, so to speak...

With all your experience, both personal and professional, what advice would you give to a single mother trying to raise men in this society today with all the obstacles a young man has to deal with? Before you get to that question, do you also find there are more Blacks and Latinos in the prison and jail population?

Yes...it's way more...it's very disproportionate.

Okay, let's go back to the question...I just wanted to get that in there.

Okay, I would say to her, first of all – be strong...know that it's a huge responsibility. I don't think people understand how much a responsibility it is raising a male...if you're raising a male, you're raising a leader of this generation. You have to be set in your tone to teach him the things he needs to survive. I would put pressure on her to find any positive male role models that's around you; whether it be your brothers, men in your church, pastor, neighbor...any positive role model...lean towards them... don't be afraid to ask for help. A lot of women take on this attitude about "I don't need a man, I can do it myself." We were created to be in relationships with other people. If that wasn't true...God would have just made one and that would have been it. We were created to survive, build relationships, and help one another out.

And that's the one thing that is missing from the black community - we don't bond, we don't believe in helping each other and loving each other unconditionally. Any other community, they do it – the Asian community, the Native American community does...every other race or group of people will bond together...black people, we won't do it. We always find a way to be to ourselves...we'll support what they're doing...but we won't support our own, and I can't grasp that...I don't understand...I really don't.

It's funny, you hit the nail on the head...one of the things I keep coming across in my research and discussions with women is this prevalent attitude of, I don't need anyone to help me raise my son...it seems they are afraid or too prideful to reach out for help. I feel you do!

That's just like, if I wanted to build a house, I know that I, personally, could not build a house, I couldn't even start with the foundation of the house...I haven't been trained...I'm not a carpenter...I don't even know where to start! The best thing I can do is read books; educate myself on how to start the foundation. So I say that to say this: as a woman who knows nothing about being a man...you may know a lot about dealing with men, being in relationships with men, but not actually being one...thinking like one... operating as a man...taking a leadership position like a man...I mean, you can take a leadership position, but I'm talking about like a man! Teaching a boy to be a man...how can you say, that you don't need any help? It's the same thing as me saying I don't need any help building this house, and I'm aware I know nothing about building this house, or me getting a brand new Mercedes Benz and trying to work on it – when I know nothing about how to work on it. The only thing I could do if I take that attitude is to destroy everything that I have. There's no way I can make it better. The only thing I'm going to do is destroy if I take an attitude of I can do it myself, I can fix it myself – no you can't! You haven't been trained, you don't know anything about it; I've owned a lot of cars, but if I get up under the hood and act like I know what I'm doing – I'm going to tear it apart.

You have a generation of women that are trying to build and handle this complex thing called man without any instructions, without any teaching, without any tutoring. Whatever you believe in your higher power sets forth guidelines. If you're a Muslim, it's the Koran; if you're a Christian, it's the Bible...or it may be the Torah...whatever you believe in it's your guideline and that's what you lean on. Me, I'm a Christian, so I lean on the Bible. My mother and my grandmother, they leaned on the Bible to help as a guide, but they still needed those men for the practical things. The Bible is not going to teach you how to change the oil in your car. I listen to women my age, maybe a little younger or older, complain that men aren't like they used to be...you don't know how to change your oil, you don't know how to change your tire...I get in my car and I see these young kids and the girl gets out and she pumps the gas and you watch? You call Triple A because your tire is flat...come on, dude, change the tire...but it's simply because they haven't been taught. Their uncles and their granddaddies are not around.

It's all learned behavior because it's not natural, not normal. It's always been my natural inclination to take care of the women; take care of my mother, my sister...I have three daughters, wife, a sister, mother...I even have a female dog...I have a lot of women that are around me...it's always been something that's come natural to me. I have a lot of uncles, but a lot of them have had girls, a lot of my cousins were female...those I'm closer to are females...so I've developed this inclination to be their protector. Some people want to argue that if a man is raised by a bunch of women that there's a chance he may be feminine; I never got that...that just was never me...I don't buy that because I was that guy that had all the female cousins...I'm protecting my cousins from my friends. All my friends wanted to come over and talk to my female cousins. I just hung around them, but I always drew that line. Okay, y'all playing with the dolls, then I'm going to have to get the radio control car, we can play together, but I'm not about to play with the dolls...y'all about to play hopscotch, well I'm going to have to find some friends and play hide and go seek. It didn't have that effect on me. I was around them but it didn't make me want to be like them.

But you had the balance of male influence too.

Oh, yeah...they set the precedent. There were times I grabbed the doll and was playing with it and my uncle and father would say 'hold up – that's not for you – that's for them (the girls)!' That early chastisement and being on me about that – it only took one time for that to happen. My uncle told me, "Don't you ever play with a doll and I don't care if it is a man doll (I was playing with the Ken Doll) - you don't play with them!" and that was it for me. And I listened because I looked up to him and he was one of my uncles that was always around. You cannot convince me that it doesn't make a difference when there's not a prominent male figure around. As I got older, my dad, he ended up getting married (mother and father were not married when I was born), and when he had children with his wife, our relationship was not as strong, mainly because of whatever feeling she had toward my mother. To keep the peace, he pretty much just said 'I'll try to split my time between each family'. But it was tough because I was used to seeing him every day...and so that was a dramatic shift; so as a result of that, it took a toll on our relationship. As I got older I spent less time with him, which led me to gravitate towards my friends. When I started gravitating more towards my friends there's another aspect that starts to evolve here – I'm starting to do things like experiment with smoking, stealing, and doing all kinds of stuff and getting influenced...I feel like I'm older now...too old to be hanging out with my uncles, I wanted to hang out with my friends...without my dad's guidance...he was still around, but spent less time with me. I'm now spending all that time with my friends. It began to change me.

Our relationship changed and I started looking for guidance from my friends. During those high school and college years you start experimenting, with the girls, etc. I'm starting to fly. The one thing I didn't do was stray from what I was taught. Even though I was on my own and I was doing stuff, every decision I made was completely my own decision. If I did something stupid, it wasn't because I didn't know; it was because I chose not to do the right thing.

One of those things I was taught was never to put your hands on a woman... they're physically weaker.

And where did you learn that from – the male or female side of the family – or both?

I learned it from both sides. My family was pretty religious and that's what we were taught. My mom and my dad taught me that. Once I got older and decided to develop a relationship between God and myself it was my pastor who assumed that role of my father. It transitioned...it took a while for it to transition, because I was in the streets for a long time. But once I decided that I wanted to do the right thing, settle down and get married, have kids, get myself together, it was another male that influenced my life. Even now if I have an issue and I need somebody to give me advice, I don't take that attitude 'I don't need help'; I go to my pastor and ask for guidance. If I'm struggling with something, dealing with my wife or family, or financial decisions, I go to somebody that I trust. My wife can tell me something 10 times, but I could go to my pastor and he could tell me something similar, but it just sounds different coming from another man. I may hear something from another black male, but somehow it just hits me differently than if it had come from my mom. She could be saying the same thing, but it just sounds different coming from another male.

This book is awesome; I really think it's going to be awesome! When John told me about it, it was so ironic that we met, because here we are a long way from home, in Jamaica, and this is conversation, barbershop talk that we have all the time. And me being in a position in which I can give insight and talking about how important it is. I tell these men in prison, 'Listen, man, you may not have a good relationship with your mother or child, but don't let that stop you from being active in these male's lives'. And the females too – that's a serious problem. But as far as addressing the males, I tell them 'make sure that you've got a relationship...even if it's just to talk. Let them know you're available. Just being available may be enough...just the fact that you avail yourself to be a part of your son's life...hey I know it's been rocky, I know I haven't been there for the last few years...'

Some of these guys in prison...their kids were babies when they left...the only thing they know about their dad is coming to visit them and letters. The prison system has allowed them to be able to email their families. But my point is, the sons basically do not know them, they know of them...they were small when they left...some of these guys in these federal cases are serving mandatory sentences – 15, 20, 35 years depending on the charge... so when they get out they have a chance to be with them for the first time. You can only do so much. It's never too late, nevertheless, to build a relationship. Why not try to be in their life every day that you can?

For that mother – decide what's more important – you and their father's relationship or establishing something, or allowing a relationship to kindle, that can set the tone of that child's life you brought into the world. Because as parents, we live our lives...a lot of people have their kids young...but once you bring a life into the world, you are no longer the concern... your concern is that child, that life. As a mother you must establish that relationship with the father, that connection...and if the father doesn't want to be a part of that, you can't make them do that...I understand... but you can lean on someone that's close, like a grandfather. Find a male, somebody...you can't tell me that there's nobody that will step in and help out. It's hard for me to imagine that. If you go somewhere...

I just did that not too long ago...a young lady that came to the church had 3 sons and her sons lost their father. She came to the church and said 'I'm at my wit's end, I don't know what to do, I pray that the Lord change their hearts'...one was in a gang...the younger one was following his brother's steps and he was starting to get involved in gang activity...and so when I heard her story I said, 'I got girls, I've worked in an environment where I've seen young men like this all the time in the system. I've got to get this kid before he does something stupid'. This coach in a boxing club trained kids for free...so I made myself available with the guy and I took the classes too. And the other kids who came to class did so because their mom made them, but the one I took under my wing was really good. And I saw that he had something in him...so I took the time... I got a cell phone and I checked on him every day...he would call me whenever stuff was going wrong. And, I would go to his fights.

I developed a relationship with him. I got with his mom and she would call me any time he was doing wrong...she might say 'I had to put him out of the house because he came home late or was smoking'...so I would call him and ask 'where are you at?' 'Are you going to class?' I might see him walking and I'd pick him up and take him to training/practice. I'd pick up some food for him...it nurtured him so much that he started working, paying bills for his mom...and I saw him grow, and that was big. That was my personal investment and a chance to see what I could do. And it was great to see a mother who was not afraid to say; 'I don't know what else I can do. Somebody please help me.' And it just took me standing up. Other guys doing the same thing...doing something as simple as taking them to school...taking them to look for a job...taking them to eat...going to stores in the mall...offering encouragement...talking about girls. I would give him money, 20-40 dollars and tell him to take his girlfriend out...but it's bigger than the $40, it's the fact that you cared enough...it meant a whole lot to him...and it all came from this mother saying 'I need help'. She could say to him – 'get a job, you need to stop being lazy and get out there' – but to him it just sounds like nagging. But I might say to him – 'C'mon player, what are you doing? No girl is going to get with you if you ain't got no job!' And he'll listen.

Some of these guys don't want their mom to know about what they're doing with girls. They might think she's going to get on them, whereas a guy like me is going to give it to them real. No, I'm not going to validate you having sex without getting married – that's not what I'm going to do... but if you are, be smart about it, don't start getting these girls pregnant...if you get of age, of course, it's your decision, but I can give you advice...I can tell you, you are going to make your life a whole lot harder than it needs to be...no kids...you can take care of yourself...you don't have to spend a lot of money. I'm able to talk to them and deal with them on that level and it makes a big difference as opposed to them talking with their mom or a woman about it.

Before a woman learns how to do her own hair, they had to let someone else do it...whether it was their mom, whether it was their aunt, grandmother or anyone else...they had to be taught how to do that...it wasn't something automatic...you didn't just learn how to do your own hair...you have to practice, mess up a couple of times, burn your forehead trying to curl it yourself...you've made mistakes and you're going to...you're not going to be perfect. To me, you need help. So why would you take something like your son's life and try to think you can raise a complex being on your own? A man is complex...is designed so intricately...all men are designed to be leaders. We were put in the position to take dominion over the whole earth...over everything...nothing is higher than a man, a human being... so it's an important responsibility, especially when a boy is young because they are constantly learning.

It amazes me how smart my kids are...because I look at them...they're in that learning stage...whatever the program, they can pick it up...they can use an iPad; they can use a computer better than I can. One daughter is 9, the other is 6, and they are so advanced than I was at that age...the way that they learn...everything is digital – TV, music...sometimes you've got to slow them down...you're not grown, slow it down...sometimes you have to calm them down.

In dealing with the males in the prison system, I've observed there is a tremendous amount of homosexuality, I feel, that manifested from being more emotional...having those homosexual tendencies. Am I a believer that you can be born this way? It's possible...you can be born with any type of identity issue, especially a gender issue when you're talking about chromosomes...disease, or deformity...but specifically in the prison system, now that the guys are younger and they are more emotional, they tend to take on this aura of female. There's a lot of gang violence and the reason guys join gangs is because of a fear...

It's natural for women to gather together, to flock together kind of like sheep...sheep huddle and gather together to stay warm. For men, it's natural to be hunters and we go out on our own, especially when we're talking about the alpha and beta...the alpha male roams alone...and with these guys in the prison they develop this thing in which they're needy... they need validation from other men...it's crazy! Women often need validation from other women...you know how they are...when a woman compliments another woman it's like, 'Oh girl, your hair looks good' and they compliment each other, feel on each other's boobs, and press each other's hair and so on...it's the same thing with these dudes in prison who have been raised by these women – this is what they see – they don't have a male in the home to show them any different. So they hear this conversation and they talk like a female – even gossip like many females. It's not really in a man's nature to gossip and do stuff like that. And when these guys join a gang, they do it for protection, out of fear...fear of being different...and a lot of those guys can shoot, but they can't fight. I've been doing this for a long time...I've had to go one on one with a lot of dudes and I'll expose them...you may have done murder, but you can't fight...they don't even know how to take a punch or throw a punch. Picking up a gun because you are fearful...you were raised by that woman, but you've never been taught how to square up, how to take one...these guys they will pick up a gun quick because they are emotional and when you have a male that's emotional becomes dangerous...an emotional male is a dangerous thing because his rage can be vengeful...an angry woman might cut your tires up...you have some women that might kill you, but an angry man who wants to get past that point is emotional and doesn't realize the repercussions or the consequences of what he is doing becomes very dangerous. And when I've talked to these guys after they've done their time and all they say, "Man, I have never done anything like that before, and that guy was just running off at the mouth and I just blanked..."

This guy has not learned how to handle his emotions, he hasn't been taught how to think rationally, your emotions conquer you – that's what women do emotionally...they start crying, they're ready to walk out and leave a man or a marriage they've been in for 20 years because the guy doesn't look at them the same way. Guys, we do things that make sense - man I'm not about to leave my wife...we think about it...we don't allow our emotions to take over...some men do...but generally speaking women are more emotional than men. When you have a generation of emotional men with guns in their hands, and drug-induced...you've got a problem... and it spills over into the problems we have now...law enforcement. A lot of these police officers...I'm willing to bet you, if you really look into their backgrounds you'll find weren't raised by strong men.

It all stems from that fear. Believe it or not, I talk to a lot of cops, because we have relationships, and I have many friends who are officers, and I tell them a lot of stuff is happening because of that fear...police fear a lot of black men because they know that he'll do anything at any given time, generally speaking; not all black men...they have it set in their mind, they don't know them, so they don't know what they'll do...it's a distrust.

I hate to compare men to dogs, but for instance, I own a pit bull...some of my friends don't come to my house anymore because I have a pit bull. The dogs have been stereotyped. But the truth of the matter is, if you raise a pit bull right, there is no way that he will attack a person. My dog is the scariest-looking dog on this earth - she looks vicious, but she's a pussycat...I raised her not to be aggressive...so I feel safe with her around my kids...I know guys that fought dogs for a living and they will tell you, if you don't make it a gang dog, it will not be that type of dog. It's not really their nature to be that way. A Chihuahua or smaller dogs - they will bite you.

My point is, men can do anything - athletically, scientifically - but it all depends on how you raise that person...that young man...whether he's going to be vicious or victorious...

RESPONDENT #4 (Deputy Sheriff/Corrections Officer)

Family Background

I'm the oldest...and when our parents divorced I got thrown under the bus as becoming a bill payer and helping her to survive for my other siblings...she started stressing out to me about bills that have to be paid, otherwise the utilities and other things will be turned off, and other stuff... schoolwork was thrown on the backburner and I had the concerns of a grown man at about 13 or 14 years old...cutting grass, bagging groceries, walking to work. I could tell the big shift when my father was there because he was always around and I could tell the big shift because we were snatched away from him...we went from her being stable to when she was like an emotional rollercoaster...she couldn't take the burden that a man could take...a man could take crap on his job and still come back and run the household...I remember seeing the difference in how the bills were handled after the split and how weak and vulnerable my mom was...I would see her in an emotional state and how she would take it out on us... and I don't know if it's in relation to do with material stuff and what you can't have, children...like my dad didn't deal with you on a material level, trying to get you the fancy stuff...he pretty much hit you with – 'Cut the grass' – and we would...and if you asked for something you weren't going to get any more...my dad would say you have to learn how to ride the bike before you ask for one. On the female side you could ask for stuff but you didn't have to do anything for it. She'd just give it to you because you're her 'baby'. I could manipulate her by becoming emotional myself...many females are like these guys in prison, they become more emotional...and with the visitations in prisons, there were a number of females...in very few of them would their dad come...I'd hear all that complaining as they would explain to their mothers...it's different when you have a man in the picture...you have to deal with the authority figure.

At that time when I was growing up, some of my friends had never seen their dad...all of them had this problem with authority...if you got a problem with authority, right away that will run you into law enforcement, prison system...the father figure is that authority figure...right away you've got to recognize that you're not running anything and somebody else is running things, you know what I'm saying, they're going to delegate authority...so once you are confident enough you can make decisions along with that same sensible line...I can tell when someone has passed on a sensible, like a four-legged stand...you can't pull out one of the legs and expect it to stand up...so he gave us a sensible...like in the hood people will say when you are working for the white man people will say you are a sucker...when you're working for your dad, you're working because it's the responsible thing to do...and if you want something...he'll take you to go and get it and show you how to get it...there's no other trickery. Working with my dad, things were told to me in more detail...he taught me that a job is how you get the seed money to get things you want, and how to do things such as starting your own business and getting other things that you want like a house, car, etc. He talked about how not to put everything on your back, how to save money, and put some back... a lot of stuff.

Even when I was working in the prison system, I used to talk to the young black men and I would tell them how much stronger I am than you...I'm built stronger than you because I was raised from my dad, my granddad, and his dad; I have all their wisdom poured into me...I've got years of wisdom in my...I don't even see choices the way you see it...

Even though my parents got divorced, my father was still in our lives; more so talking to me mostly because I'm the oldest – he would tell me take care of your mom, look out for your brothers and sisters...me and your mother are not going to be together...hell, I didn't know what was going on. I'd see my father periodically during the summertime, but when I needed him many times he was not around. I might have some problems in school or I'd get into a fight with some knuckleheads and then I didn't have anybody but my mom...day-to-day, no he wasn't there...but I could see him every summer and that would offer my mother a break. Mothers love you and do for you, but they don't give you enough information to work with. It's a hard thing to say about your parents.

How did you handle puberty at this young age of your life?

I pretty much talked to my dad during the summer months when we were with him. His family structure was pretty much holding us together as a family from a distance. So my aunt would call us, they would send us shoes, we would come down and get hand-me-downs from my other cousins. They would always ask us how's your mama doing...always into our personal business...looking back, that made a lot of sense in terms of where we were at and asking about how the kids and family were doing, especially when you're dealing with change ...watching out for each other... and doing what you're supposed to do...because after that, we were able to show we made good choices without my dad around. A lot of kids without fathers aren't able to do that.

Having an older brother like me that got to spend a lot of time around my dad...my other younger brother-kind of mimicked my choice-making. If I don't get into any trouble, it didn't make any sense for them to get into any trouble. If I'm working with mom on a sensible basis on a job like bagging groceries and giving her half my check; when they got a job, they started giving their money to her. We tried to keep the whole family from falling into any cracks. At times I did feel like a big burden was thrown on me. When my mom used to cry on me...that just broke me all the way down...I didn't know if she was trying to manipulate me. It gave me a guilt trip...I could never have anything...I needed to put them first. I couldn't have a new car or new clothes because I'd feel guilty and knew they had to come first. I was kind of never sort of happy. When I had a girlfriend, I would buy her something, but I knew my family needed something – I always had in my mind that they had the greater need. I eventually grew out of it...I knew it wasn't my calling to be the head of the household...I'm designed that way, but I didn't feel like I had earned that right...I was thrown into it.

It sounds like your mother talked to you about the problems she had at your young age.

My mother had emotional problems, financial problems, boyfriend problems, stuff like that. And then it becomes a cycle of manipulation in which parents start using the stuff to manipulate their children. My brother makes money, I work and make decent money, my sister makes money and then it becomes a cycle of manipulation with the kids using lots of drama and drawn-out situations...that's my side of the circle of the wheel. The other guys that I see, their parents do the same thing, but instead these guys try to help them out by selling drugs, trying to get money the wrong way. When the female breaks down on them you'll hear them say 'I got to do what I got to do'...and if you ask what's going on they'll say, 'Well, my mom is on drugs and I'm trying to take care of my brothers and sisters – man, I've got to do what I do out there.' That type of failure from one or both of the parents really drives them crazy...it really drives the person crazy left trying to hold the family intact. It leads to them making bad choices about school, their pride, their ethics...girls start prostituting, start selling dope, and if you talk to them about it, a lot of them start talking about the family stuff that is pressuring them. The man is a vital piece of the family structure, he holds the binding part together...he can bind it...the daughter can penetrate stuff. It even penetrates when a girlfriend brings a boyfriend home...she's not going to bring a boy home smoking weed or cigarettes, she won't do that if an authority figure is there.

It loses its binding...it unravels if a father figure is not present. It doesn't unravel at first, but it starts unraveling at all angles and hitting all individuals – from an economic point of view – because you know you're most stable when you have two incomes...when that one income goes it produces instability...when it deteriorates like your faith and your social and income it erodes the fabric of your entire household – if she (the mother) is the head of the household, she is struggling. The way our household ran, whoever made the most money was the head...if someone was working at the post office at a young age that person was the one everyone leaned on...my tire went out, my brakes went out – that's who you'd go to...

Growing up did you know a lot of people who were in single-parent homes?

In my observation a lot of people were married when I came along. And they stayed married and when I got a little older and we moved from Macon to the big city, I started to see a lot more single families...we came from the country and there, most of the people stayed married. When we came to the big city I started noticing a bunch more single females and kids running wild everywhere...kids being left at home alone...stuff thrown out on street corners like nobody cared. And I was told to stop waving at people and speaking and saying hi to them. We found ourselves in a whole different world.

When did you become involved in law enforcement?

Right after I served time in the military I got involved in law enforcement in 1994...I worked for the D.A. in Brooklyn, NY...I came back and worked for the Dept. of Corrections in Georgia – I was an instructor in the boot camp program. I left that and I worked for the City of Atlanta in the jailing

John P. Dennis

system where I made a lot more money because it was a huge jail system... they had a big layoff and then I did a little factory work until it slowed down. Now I'm back in law enforcement on the sheriff's side of the fence. Before, I was on the side where they were incarcerated, now I'm on the side where they're going INTO incarceration. I'm going back and forth to your house 10-20 times because you're doing stuff in high school, you're stealing from Walmart, you're causing problems with your parents, and after you've gotten older you finally catch a charge worthy enough for you to go to prison...now there's no stopping you from going to prison...except some kind of influence or father figure that can instill fear in you like our parents did with us...fear of God Almighty...

In my research and discussion I find a disproportionate amount of men and women coming from single-parent homes – have you found that to be the case?

Yes.

What characteristics did you find most typical of those people?

They tend to be more emotional, more combative, unreasonable, they're putting it on the line. If it was more typical of having a dad, you'd say that ain't worth fighting for...let him have it...if he wants it that bad, let it go...they stole from you, it ain't worth the battle. They are on this 'somebody's testing them, disrespecting them' and all the other stuff. If you find somebody is disrespecting you, does that mean you feel somebody has to fear you? To them it means, if you disrespect me, you have to fear me. 90% of the fights I go through it's always because someone says 'he disrespected me' – so I say to them 'so you're telling me since he disrespected you, he now has to fear you?!' Is disrespect a sign of fear? Does that word mean you need to fear me? With a dad you don't have to go into all that stuff about you need to fear me...So there's some kind of breakdown in communication. So you take these guys and they design their own system in the prison without a male presence and they translate it back into the street...they put that same code back on the street, like no snitching...so they run a whole system...remember, he had to sell drugs to take care of his family...so he ends up developing the code of a drug dealer...so he goes to prison, he comes back out on the street and now he tries to control the whole block – socioeconomic power – and now the police try to straighten stuff out, but now they can do anything...now they're running the prison rules on the street...and making sure no one can snitch...again, you're disrespecting me – you need to fear me.

So you're saying you believe there is a correlation between the emotionalism and fear that we see from a male raised by a single mother that carries on in the prison system?

Yes. When you look at my uniform you see me as an authority figure. Most of the whites will see me as an authority figure and say, "Yes sir, no sir..." and go on about their business. Most of my folks will say, "Yeah...what? What's up?" The recognition of authority is distorted...the authority goes back to 'you're disrespecting me' – you need to fear me for them to have some type of authority over someone. I tell them you have to go by brainpower and gaining knowledge. You're passing on the wrong knowledge of how to get drugs...how to get over laws and not do time...you got minors selling drugs because you know they don't do time...your focus is wrongly on how to beat the system – that's the mentality I'm often dealing with. You can't ultimately survive on how to beat the system.

Do you find a much larger percentage of blacks and other minorities in the prison?

Yes. Definitely. My dealings with the law enforcement system is that they don't get as many breaks as other groups because my feelings are that oftentimes the ones giving the breaks are the same ones they are giving the breaks to. People tend to sympathize with those that look like them vs. someone who doesn't. It's a fact of life. We can make it sound good, like yeah, everyone is equal...but the fact is, someone of the same color sways them. It's like me, when I go dealing with some black folks, I understand what they're talking about when she says, I can't do nothing with him, and his daddy is locked up and so and so...I understand what she's talking about. Just those words right there translate my whole childhood...my neighbors, everybody that has been through it and made it out the other end. We can interpret the whole thing. I know exactly what's wrong with him by her saying it. Being a person of the same background and seeing her in the same struggles my mom was in with kids and no man around. Where they are living at is not that nice, beat up car, they're probably getting a free lunch at school, no clothes...I can see the whole struggle the kid is going through. He is probably mad at school, he doesn't have the clothes that the other kids have, probably ain't making the grades, he's distracted and comes home angry with those emotions and lack of and not having enough of. I've been through it so I understand what he's going through. But I'm older now and realize my mom gave me everything I needed. I don't know how society put this burden on these children that make them have to steal or fight for these Jordan's and stuff like that.

Did guys in prison talk to you about not having a father?

Oh yeah...they'd say, [Officer T] why are you always telling us this stuff? And I would say, my Daddy and Granddaddy would tell you what they went through, you don't have to go through none of that...a school bus comes to your neighborhood for free...you don't have to put any gas in it...they will take you to school for free...feed you...educate you...bring you back home and all that's required of you is to come back the next day. What you need to do is keep your freaking mouth closed and do what you have to do to graduate. Once you graduate you can go somewhere else free to go where you can educate yourself...go into the military...you can have all these things if you go along with the system and the program...that's what they would tell you. My dad would tell you why would you come to the prison and work for free picking up trash for 10-15 years and you won't take a job bagging groceries, or cleaning bathrooms and doing toilets; yet you're living in a prison where you have to use the bathroom in the open and you can't enjoy a wife, kid, and family all because you want to sell drugs...your choices are messed up. You got two wires on top of each other because you made some very bad choices.

And they would just sit there and listen. And one would say, We hear you... I've been here 5 years and I've never heard none of that...and I was too stupid and he'll say to me I've been looking for knowledge like that – no one has ever talked to me about that. And one guy says to me, "Hey officer, you don't make but $20,000 a year, you don't make no money..." and I tell him, "Listen, man, I've been working since I was a young man for 30 years and I've made over $600,000, how much did you make selling dope for your 2 years' time and then got locked up?" I'm just talking...but I tell them, I've got enough money if I had to take a man's life I could get myself a good lawyer and get a year's probation...You're in the state prison...I tell him, you can't even beat a drug charge...all the big guys go to the fed prison...you're not even educated. They've got guys hired with bachelor's and master's degrees that catch you guys...it's like catching fish in a net... you're not even smart enough...you don't even know the system...you're trying to learn the system backwards...you're trying to learn it through these jailhouse lawyers what you did wrong...and how to cut your dope... where you're going to hide it...they've got guys out there with bachelor's and master's degrees, four or five organizations...they talk to real lawyers and stuff.

I try to make them understand it's a lose-lose situation. They ask me, 'Well, how do we get on the right track?' I tell them when I grew up and as I got older and started buying houses and making money, I found out in my culture that myths, rumors, and lies are viewed as the truth...everybody saying the white man is doing this or that is not the truth...it may be relevant, but you can't use that and start going crazy with it as an excuse. You have to look at it in moderation. Saying I ain't going to do a white man's job or join a white man's army is crazy – I say to them, 'what's wrong with you guys – have you lost your mind? Are you watching too much "Boyz in the Hood"?' That's entertainment.

When you're talking to a real man...there's a difference than when you're talking to your homeboy. I'm a husband, so I tell them; I'm going to talk to you in a different way. As your father I'm going to give you a greater insight on it.

That's why when you break down the social parts of it the conversation is so different. I can always tell my brother, John, so what? But when my dad is talking to both of us, he is talking some way deep stuff! He was talking about marriage before we even got married...he was talking about housing, banking, stuff we knew nothing about... we're thinking, man he doesn't know what he's talking about, but we found out later he was absolutely right and knew 15 years before we even got there.

What I encountered in the prisons is that their situation was so jacked up to reverse it. I had to start from the beginning. I ended up criticizing their parents, stating 'you're a victim of this, but this is how you get out of that and your associations'. I had to end up tearing down his whole damn structure to call him out – I'd say 'this is who you are...and that's not a good person! You're a monster!' I'd say, 'your girlfriend sees you as a deadbeat dad...your children never see you around'. I said to him 'why are you worrying about how much money I'm making when you need to worry about you? This is what YOU are!' A lot of people haven't looked at themselves in the mirror. That's what your dad will do for you – give you that good shot early...

Advice to give a single mother raising a son

That young man needs to be around other men that will help translate what he's going to be...we need to pick out somebody we want him to be like...does that make sense? It's up to her, and his and her benefit to be around somebody like that, who is positive...it can be an older guy that fishes all the time...or the neighbor two houses down that's retired from the military...someone home every day who cuts his grass that he can spend time with. It's a time management...you're going to have to put me (the young man) around somebody that I want to be like. Not a drug dealer or hustler or anyone talking crazy to me.

We've got guys on all these different levels – some guys love cars, others like music, some like to fish like me, some love sports...you see a guy who is quiet and you mention sports and he can't stop talking about college football, etc., whatever is his interests. Some guys want to talk about

141

women all the time...some want to talk about money, starting their own business, working two jobs, etc.

Jolene Swain (Clinical Professor, Field Education, MSW)

Completed documentary in 2013.

Tell me a little more about your background and how you got to where you are in regards to your consulting work on mothers raising sons.

I became a single mom when my son was two, he's 27 now...and I was raised with all sisters so I had no clue what it would be like to raise this male child. I didn't know what I was doing, what I was in for, etc., but I knew enough as a social worker and it was always going to be my plan to send my son to therapy when he started to ask why my dad wasn't here. And that happened about age 5. He started therapy literally at age 5 because I wanted someone to help explain what the issues were. His dad was an alcoholic so he had an addiction problem. We were college sweethearts and we got married...

Do you mind if I ask if his dad is still around?

He is, but he was inconsistent in his life, mainly because of his issues with his mother, which I think led to some of his addictions...and the fact that he has an addiction has caused him to be inconsistent in my son's life. So for the most part, there were big chunks of time when his dad was not around.

So from the time he was 5-8 we were in therapy to help him wrap his brain around that you are going to be raised by a single mom, your dad has an addiction problem...we always tried to be honest about that...and this is how your life is going to be. It all comes back to LOSS. There's always going to be this loss in life of not having his dad there. After we stopped therapy at 8 I told him you will probably need to go back...most likely at age 13 you're probably going to feel the loss of your dad not being in your life again! But this time you'll need to go to a male and I want it to be an

African American male. As it worked out, one Sunday at church when he was around 11 he said to me I want to go back to therapy because I'm really angry at my dad. So we went back to that therapist and she referred us...

I'm sorry to interrupt you, but that's pretty amazing that he recognized that need for himself.

Well, you've got to remember, I've been talking to him every day about things and he's been to therapy so he has no fear of it. He knows going to therapy doesn't mean he's crazy...it's his opportunity to talk about his feelings...now I'm not saying every mom can get there, but what I am saying is this is how WE got here.

So at the age of 11 the initial therapist referred us to her supervisor who worked with boys. He is in the documentary and his name is Michael Hughes. He started seeing Jared and he still sees him till this day because he's still dealing with his loss. It takes a long time to become a man and I can't do it because I'm not a man. I have my brother-in-law who's been there for him, but he lives in Atlanta so as consistent as he was, he just wasn't physically here. Michael, in many ways, ended up becoming his surrogate father and mentor and life coach...he still wants to see him even after he went away to college...they continued to Skype and talk on the phone...at any point he could have stopped and said I'm done with this relationship, but he still continues to do it because he still needs a man guiding him through his relationships, the things I cannot do...and I'm not supposed to be doing it...he's a young man now.

Boys need two things: they need a maternal love from the ages of 0-10, and then they move into being mentored and coached by men. Then they have to find a romantic love...so I can't be in his life anymore. It's like I explained in the documentary, as mothers we have to let go. But generic to all boys and mothers is this special bond...in which they do become that intimate couple. They're not aware of this, it's all subconscious. A mother will literally hold on and not let her son go and that then becomes the problem. And the boy becomes her psychological husband. And it becomes so dysfunctional in the way it plays out. He can never be a REAL man if he has this emotional attachment to his mother that he can't let go.

So I had to educate myself and one of the people I quote a lot, Michael Gurian, who came out of the Harvard Institute of Medicine, is a psychologist who has been doing all this research on boys...he has this book on "The Wonder of Boys" on which he talks about the role of the mother from 0-10 and what she needs to do. And when I read that I thought, oh my gosh, this is the work that I need to do, so I started doing a lot of reading and researching. I was already a certified parent educator, but I strongly felt I needed to start educating these moms out here because we're the ones that are messing up our boys! We are infantilizing them...we don't let them grow up because we won't let go!

And something that is specific to African American moms is how our sons suffered during slavery, that intergenerational trauma, historical trauma – we still hold on even more and it's a reality to this day....because of Jim Crow and through what's going on now – our boys aren't safe! As a result we really lock on to them. Therefore they never have an opportunity to grow up.

And then there's another piece. Most single moms have a really difficult time. Boys between 8-10...maybe 12, start really feeling their oats...they get very powerful in their presence because they are coming into their own. Some of these moms get really scared and they don't know how to treat the boundaries. And then by the time they are 15 and 16 the boy can go out there and really make some money and bring it back in the house to help support the family...but then she really loses a lot of power because now you've got the son in a role that he's not supposed to be in...so she really cannot get the boundaries with him when he's bringing in money to support the family...be it through drugs, working at 7-11, be it through whatever...now he has too much power...and there's no adult man there to keep him at bay. So this is what happens. And now they've become this couple because they are really operating like a husband and wife in a sense, but obviously they can't cross that boundary of a sexual relationship, so he goes out in the world and has sex, but he always comes back to his mama. That's why we're getting more single parents – do you see what I'm saying? The pattern has been set.

We keep perpetuating the problem because we won't let go. That mother should really say: Uh, uh, you can't have a baby out there and live here! You should be with your family and if you're going to start a family you need to think about loyalty and commitment! But she doesn't because he's serving a purpose for her. He's her emotional support and may be her financial support. So we're setting our sons up not to go out and create their own healthy families. We don't know it because it's subconscious. We need to educate ourselves about this. And don't get me wrong, I think the book is great, but we also need parent education sessions. We need to be a support to each other in order to really let go. You need to be single moms raising boys with an understanding of how this whole developmental phenomena plays itself out. This is the Oedipus Complex. That's what it is. I did the documentary to jumpstart things, to show that there should be educational workshops for women and single mothers and also a call out to men to be prepared to be there, to help us mentor and coach our sons in a positive way because that's what we need. If we're going to release them, we need a male community that's going to be there to receive them. And that's, again, the reason why I did this documentary...mothers need to be educated and it helps to come from another woman to tell her you can't teach your son how to become a man, because you're not a man.

I'm so glad to hear you say that because when John and I started discussing the concept of this book, with many women there was a defensiveness and resistance there.

Let me tell you, when I got out of that Center I got tomatoes and eggs on my face because they were like, what? Black women are socialized to think of themselves in this circumstance as the man and a woman; mother and a father – no you're not! It's not true! We have to stop thinking that way! We are not both! And sometimes I'm not very popular because I tell women that. And I am not going to stop saying it! That's been my struggle or challenge in getting parent education off the ground regarding this because African American women don't want to hear it. The attitude is, I can do it alone!

And why do you think that is?

It's because of their socialization. And the other piece is, my feeling, is that they are doing it alone...it's like, I don't want to hear about myself because I am doing it...my son may have 2 or 3 kids out there with a woman(s) but I'm letting him stay here with me...because maybe I'M not emotionally happy... my son makes me happy...and I'm never going to embrace that woman he is with...I don't like her. And this is what is said instead of embracing that woman and trying to work with her. So I think it's a lot of that, I've talked about it with women and they totally shut down. And I know, because I'm a social worker, you feel that way because you're doing it. You're doing exactly what I'm saying you can't do. It's not the healthiest way for your son to do it – but they don't want to hear it! You are doing your son such a disservice...you really are...and yourself in the end. No mother wants her son not to live his life to full capacity, but that's exactly what you're doing...

When we got divorced, and even though we were in our early thirties, that's where he went...he went back home to his mother and she received him. She let him come home. Now if my son gets married and something goes wrong, I'll tell him – No, you can't come here, you cannot, so you might as well go back, try to work it out, whatever...but you can't come here. My friend, Stephanie, who was in the documentary, her ex-husband when he left her went back home to his mother. Instead of saying, NO you can't come back here – go back to your wife and kids, she still took him in. That includes the woman who was crying at the end of the documentary who said she had to try and understand that - "He's my son, not my companion." Her son had that baby and she jumped up and down screaming about him marrying that girl and I said to her, "Deborah, you cannot want your son, Joshua, to be at home with you and not with his girlfriend and baby...you raised him by yourself for the exact same reason and now you're getting ready to do it again?"

But it was really hard for her. And we're sending these messages making it too easy for them. The mom makes it too easy – cooking, washing for him...so how is he going to become a man? She's doing everything. My son went to college, but I told him you can't come back here...you're moving backwards...No! It may take a long time, I understand, and you may need some help from me, I'm happy to do that, but you can't come back here – that's too easy. We have to be able to do that with our sons: stand tall, keep the boundaries, and move them forward. And no good male figure in his life is going to support that. His therapist, my brother-in-law all are going to tell him that's not what you need to do. What? Go home to your mother??? No way! And people say to me all the time, "Awww, you put your son through college and now he can come back home..." And I tell them – no he can't! I can take care of myself. I'm not looking for my son to take care of me just because he went to college. No, I'm still the mother!

A man can't serve two women – he can't! It's like you're pulling him in two different directions. And that's why the mother has to let go around 10 or 11 because you start thinking he's your emotional peer. He's not! And boys are going to do that anyway because they feel like they should be the protector. We have to tell our sons you are not the adult here – I am! You've got to stay in your world as a mother. This is not your partner! It's your child. He shouldn't know anything about your finances, nothing about your love life, nothing. Now you can say, we're not spending any money right now, things are tight. But he should know nothing specific or the details about your finances! That's how we end up supporting them, almost psychologically, to go out there and sell drugs and stuff...and his feeling is, I've got to get money to take care of my mom.

These kids have no lack of boundaries, given too much power and authority too soon. And it's because the mother can't control the boundaries...they are afraid of the consequences. They think if I say NO, my son is going to be really mad at me. And then the son is like; I can't leave because I see my mother sitting on the couch all by herself. And it's because the mother sits there doing nothing...she has no friends, no life of her own... all she does is cry about how hard she works, and how she's talking care of you, and so on. And then the boy feels like it's something he has to do, it's his responsibility and problem. He really thinks it's something he's got to figure out. Why is she telling him? She's telling him because she wants help and he ends up spending the rest of his life trying to make her happy. And he really doesn't know how to. Again, it's a setup. The mother is the one that socializes the boy how to be in a relationship, and that's why he doesn't want to be in a committed relationship with any woman because all he hears is complaining and unhappiness and depression...and I want this and I want this, and I'm unhappy. Why would he want to find a woman of his own when he hears all this?

We perpetuate this ourselves. We become our own worst enemy in a sense because it's a setup for him never to leave and when he tries to go he comes back. We can't build healthy communities because we need men in the communities. Communities are made of families and we have almost stopped creating healthy African American families. Mainly because our men are afraid...they are commitment-phobic because they feel attached to their mothers. Their emotional relationship is with their mother. They just have a physical relationship with the women out there, but the emotional relationship is with their mother. A lot of these guys will say, "I'm not trying to marry you...you can have my baby, but I'm not trying to marry you!"

Are you doing workshops currently on this subject?

I would love to be doing workshops, but currently there is no venue for them. I've done them before and through some of my consulting work I've been doing parent education work in some of the charter schools here. I've really been focusing lately on this mother-son dynamic and I have a curriculum ready to go. I did it 4 or 5 years ago, even before the documentary came out. This stuff I'm on fire with, and when I figured it out I felt like everybody needs to know this – it's so simple. I've seen mothers say, I'm using all this stuff you've told me, and it's made all the difference in the world with my relationship with my son. It's not that they don't get it; they've just got to hear it. To be honest, John Singleton tried to say it in

Boyz in the Hood and *Baby Boy* and they tried to say it in *Jump the Broom,* but because it's Hollywood and it's all glossed over – nobody's listening. Remember when the mother released her son to the father in *Boyz* and said 'now I need you to teach him how to be a man'.

But I also want to make sure mothers understand, in releasing their son to a man, that I'm not saying to do so with a negative male either. I am saying your son needs to be released to a positive male community. That's what we need. There's simultaneous work that needs to be done – the mothers need to do their job, but the fathers need to be doing so, too. That's the reason my pastor, who is in a collaborative with your cousin, Rev. Moore, asked me to come and show my documentary to the men in the church, which is a good place to do so. A place where the boys can see real men.

The reason why it is so important to educate moms is this is a lifelong thing that plays out. And you need to understand what your role is, who you have to be, and how you have to respond to your son lifelong. And the process of letting go is lifelong. I really believe in my heart that it can make a difference. Even when I showed it to the ministers they were all saying, oh my goodness...they were impacted by it and started sharing stories, and some realized how they had played into their mothers. They're better off than many men, but they could feel the impact, too. The documentary has as much impact on the males as it does the females. They suddenly realize – she was being overbearing and she wanted me to be her psychological husband – it is an eye-opener for them as well.

What do you say to these woman authors who are telling single mothers you can be successful without recruiting male influences in your son's life?

First of all, the way our brains are wired is totally different overall. No, we are not raising these sensitive sons – that's not what we're doing. You will over-feminize them and then they will be nothing. We (women) cannot do this. To me this whole feminist movement has just messed up everything because, to me, I think: Girl, you're acting like a man...so the men get confused and they don't know their role. We're not even teaching girls to put the smash on them and that's a problem because of the whole movement. I don't need my son to get out of the car and pump my gas; I can do it myself or have the man in my life do it. And I hope his girlfriend will tell him, I'm not getting out of this car to pump gas – you do it.

The point is we've got everything twisted because we use our sons in that way – to pump our gas, wash our cars, do errands, etc. I hear from women all the time about how my son will one day take care of me and it makes me crazy! I tell them it's not his job or my expectation. I can take care of myself.

What do you tell a woman who is going through financial strife who says, but I need my son to help out the family?

That's how I started consulting. My son's father was in La La Land and I didn't receive any child support. I just got down on my knees and asked God to help me to let go of the child support and open up some financial doors for me. I tell women to look for better ways to prepare yourself, go take a class...women can co-op in terms of childcare. We need to be each other's support system, but you've got to better yourself...I went back to school and got my master's degree. I needed to be marketable because I had to take care of my son. You can sit back and moan and groan and complain, but the bottom line is – you've got to step it up and see what types of opportunities are out there.

I've had to work. And, I've had to build an emotional family here to help me take care of Jared...my family's not here...I have one sister in Atlanta, one in Chicago, my mom is in Alabama. I moved out here with my ex-husband. You need to create an emotional family, and just like they say, it takes a village, and then you need to create a village. Stop being by yourself and grumbling about what you don't have. Take care of your business. That's what you've got to do. God is not going to come down here and take care of things for you. He may provide, but you've got to do your part. I'm not saying it's easy, I know it's hard...and at the end of the day I may question if I'm doing the right things or making the right decisions, and you don't have anybody to bounce that off of...that's difficult. But if you decide to have a child, or not, because you did not make a good decision, you still have to step up to the plate and be an adult. You have to do your job. The child's job is to grow up and move away. And I'm not trying to demonize single moms, not at all.

We have to have role models and mentors, and the ability to support each other. Women are not going to get through this unless we support each other. Whether you're from Compton or Watts or wherever, it's the same challenge at the end of the day for single mothers. There may be different situations schematically, but it's all the same, same struggle. We always see those areas are targeted and other boys in more affluent areas are said to be okay – no they're not...they can fall off the cliff just like all the rest of them. I could have focused there, but I did not want to focus there because we already know that story...those males are struggling, too. We can all benefit if we all understand what it is that we are doing to our sons. We're participating in this...women need to hear it...particularly African American moms. Nonetheless, it's a generic issue. You can go out and interview White, Jewish, Latina, Asian and women of all ethnicities... they all have the same issues about their sons...that bond between mothers and sons. And you have to be really careful about it, because it's subconscious, and at times you won't realize it's there. This bond occurs with even married women, because if her emotional needs are not met, she defers them to the son. And some women don't even give their husbands half a chance... it automatically defers to the sons.

The other bad thing, and I mentioned this earlier, is that a single mom can over-feminize her son to the extent that he doesn't feel like a man on the inside, he doesn't know what his role is, he can't do anything without his mom, he's really afraid to leave her, the psychological umbilical cord has not been cut. He becomes very angry and develops a rage, and then they treat women horribly – one's a wimp and the other one is a rage- alcoholic. Unless we understand and embrace the separation in a healthy way this is what we get.

It sounds like you're putting the onus on the single mother.

Whether she's single or not, it's on the mother because there is no greater bond between a mother and son – that's why I gave that title to the documentary. However, the mother and son have to go through a healthy separation process. I don't know if this bond occurs because of the female-male biology or what...but I can tell you there is something there and if you are not careful it will overtake you with your son. At some level it's primitive or primal and it can be so destructive. I remember the first time a girl called the house my reaction was, what does SHE want? I wanted to scratch her eyes out. It's primal...and I'm saying to myself what is wrong with me? Why did I emotionally react that way? But when other mothers don't understand that, they act on it and then it's downhill. You have to bring this stuff up to a conscious level so you don't act on it and play it out. Every day you have to work on letting him go...letting him go...letting him go. And that's the truth...letting go is love. If you don't start the process at 10 when you need to, then at 15, 16, 17, and 18 you're so locked on it becomes a problem and I know it's frightening to let go. I don't ask my son to do nothing, it's too easy and he can't say no.

Boys raised by single mothers that get into trouble often have this rage, and this rage at others is really directed at their mother...you made me a wimp! You didn't let me go! You made me a punk! On the inside I feel like a punk...I don't feel like a man! I can't tell my son how men process things because I'm not a man...I don't know how it feels. From a theoretical standpoint I can explain it, but not from an emotional internal point of view because I can never know, simply because I'm not a man. That's why he needs to be talking to a man so he can process his feelings.

What advice would you give to a single mother trying to raise a son?

The first thing I'd say is, Honey, you can't do it by yourself...you're not a man so you can't do it. You may think you can, but you can't. That's an illusion and you will only do a disservice to yourself and your son.

What about the woman that says, I've seen all kinds of success stories of single women raising a son by themselves?

And I would say then show me one. You're seeing what's on the outside, but you don't know what is on the inside. I bet she's suffering and so is he. We know how to dress up and present things like everything's all good, all the time. It may look good, but it's not. People may be functioning, but they function in pain. You can start peeling away the onionskin and there it is – you'll find the real deal. That's my truth. And I want to break that myth because it totally is a myth. Money can't take care of it either. No money can compensate for my son's loss. He's still dealing with that loss of his dad being in his life.

As women nurturing a son, we need that man to say, step back, leave him alone, and let him have his space. Because the thing is, we are in the mothering business - that's what we know. My brother-in-law may tell me, leave that boy alone...and it doesn't feel good, but I know he's right and I have to step back. On that same note, my son learned how to use his therapist as his ally. I'd get in those sessions and then they'd beat me up, put me back in my place...but we need that in the business of mothering. And if you don't have that male there to say, he doesn't need all that, then we'll just get sappy all over them. And we women have to learn, I can't be all sappy around my son, he really doesn't like that. When they are 15 and 16 they just learn how to grunt. Well, I learned how to grunt too so I could communicate with them. And you've got to put some bass in your voice... you can't be wimpy; you've got to put the smash on them. And you've got to find your strength and courage and say no when necessary. I've never hit my son but I know I've been effective because he once told someone, she may be short but she can pack a punch.

But I say in the documentary, Michael Hughes saved our relationship because the mother and son naturally become entangled. He untangled us because I wasn't going to like him and he wasn't going to like me...and he wasn't going to have a happy life because he wasn't going to be able to move on.

John P. Dennis

APPENDIX 2:

FURTHER READING

BOOKS

Bassoff, Evelyn S. *Between Mothers and Sons: The Making of Vital and Loving Men*. Penguin Group, USA, 1994.

Biddulph, Steve. *Raising Boys: Why Boys are Different – and How to Help Them Become Happy and Well-Balanced Men*. Berkeley, CA: Tenspeed Press, 1997, 1998.

Bloom, Lisa. *SWAGGER: 10 Urgent Rules for Raising Boys in an Era of Failing Schools, Mass Joblessness, and Thug Culture*. New York: Think Publications, 2012.

Buchanan, Bay. *Bay and Her Boys: Unexpected Lessons I learned as a (Single) Mom*. Cambridge, MA: Da Capo Press, 2012.

Drexler, Peggy with Linden Gross. *Raising Boys Without Men: How Maverick Moms are Creating the Next Generation of Exceptional Men*. Emmaus, PA: Rodale, 2005.

Elium, Don and Jeanne Elium. *RAISING A SON: Parents and the Making of A Healthy Man*. Hillsboro, OR: Beyond Words Publishing, 1992.

Engber, Andrea and Leah Klungness. *The Complete Single Mother: Reassuring Answers to Your Most Challenging Concerns*. Holbrook, MA: Adams Media Corporation, 1995.

Gurian, Michael. *A Fine Young Man: What Parents, Mentors and Educators Can Do to Shape Adolescent Boys Into Exceptional Men*. New York: Penguin Putnam, 1998.

Gurian, Michael. *The Invisible Presence: How A Man's Relationship With his Mother Affects All his Relationships With Women*. Boston, MA: Shambhala Publications, 1994, 2010.

Gurian, Michael. *The Purpose of Boys: Helping Our Sons Find Meaning, Significance, and Direction in Their Lives*. San Francisco, CA: A Wiley Imprint, 2009.

Juffer, Jane. *Single Mother: The Emergence of the Domestic Intellectual*. New York: New York University Press, 2006.

Ludtke, Melissa. *ON OUR OWN: Unmarried Motherhood in America*. New York: Random House, 1997.

Williams, Gregalan. *Boys to Men*: Maps for the Journey. New York: Doubleday, 1997.

Wilson, James Q. *The Marriage Problem: How Our Culture Has Weakened Families*. New York: Harper Paperbacks, 2003.

INTERNET READING

"Social and Economic Characteristics of Currently Unmarried Women With a Recent Birth: 2011." http://www.census.gov/prod/2013pubs/acs-21.pdf

"Single Mother Statistics" (US Census Bureau). https://singlemotherguide.com/single-mother-statistics/

John P. Dennis

"The Moynihan Report Revisited." http://www.urban.org/Uploaded PDF/412839-The-Moynihan-Report-Revisited.pdf

"Fathers Disappear From Households Across America." http://www. washingtontimes.com/news/2012/dec/25/fathers-disappear-from-households-across-america/?page=all

"Remember the Moynihan Report?" http://www.theroot.com/articles/culture/2011/11/moynihan_report_a_critique_by_herbert_gans.html

"The Single Mom's Club – Take This Job And Love It!" http://www. huffingtonpost.com/cocoa-brown/the-single-moms-club_b_4956981.html

Single Mothers By Choice (Community Organization). http://www. singlemothersbychoice.org/about/

"Single Motherhood Increases Dramatically For Certain Demographics, Census Bureau Reports." http://www.huffingtonpost.com/2013/05/01/single-motherhood-increases-census-report_n_3195455.html

"A Generation of Men Raised By Women." http://www.artofmanliness. com/2010/12/13/a-generation-of-men-raised-by-women/

"The New Math Of The Single Mother: Why the Ranks of the Unmarried Moms Keeps Growing." http://www.politico.com/magazine/story/2014/10/the-new-math-of-the-single-mother-111842.html#.VRhFnzvF8-A

"10 Harmful Things Single Mothers Do To Ruin Their Son's Lives." http://www.gillistriplett.com/rel101/articles/harmful.html

"Can Single Women Raise Boys to Become Men?" (The Good Men Project). http://goodmenproject.com/featured-content/the-good-life-can-single-women-raise-boys-to-become-men/

"75% of Inmates are Illiterate." http://www.invisiblechildren. org/2010/11/18/75-of-inmates-are-illiterate-19-are-completely-illiterate-ruben-rosario/#sthash.cE0yqNqE.hzpcMbzV.dpbs

"Fatherless Homes Breed Violence." http://www.fathermag.com/news/2778-stats.shtml

"Fathers & Sons." https://www.psychologytoday.com/articles/200910/fathers-and-sons

The Black Star Project (Community Organization). http://blackstarproject.org/action/index.php/about-us.html

"Challenge The Status Quo: Academic Success Among School-age African-American Males (Includes statistics, forecasts, and provides policy and practice solutions)." http://www.cbcfinc.org/oUploadedFiles/CTSQ.pdf

"What Men Really Need." http://www.thompsonatlarge.com/articles/6-interviews/22-what-men-really-need.html

"Thoughts on the Rise of Single Parenthood." http://www.nationalreview.com/home-front/358990/thoughts-rise-single-parenthood-colette-moran

"72 Percent of Black Kids Raised By Single Parent, 25% Overall in U.S." http://newsone.com/1195075/children-single-parents-u-s-american/

"Single Parenthood in the United States (The Women's Legal Defense and Education Fund)." https://www.legalmomentum.org/resources/single-parent-snapshot-2014

"Coming of Age: The Importance of Male Rites of Passage." http://www.artofmanliness.com/2008/11/09/coming-of-age-the-importance-of-male-rites-of-passage/

"8 Questions for Selecting the Best Rites of Passage Programs for Your Teenager." http://soulbridging.com/8-questions-selecting-best-rites-passage-programs-teenager/

John P. Dennis

ABOUT THE AUTHOR

John Dennis was raised by a single mother and first entered the world of mentorship from being mentored himself in his early teens by his uncle. He was an honor student in school, became a USAF Air Traffic Controller, earned his Bachelor's degree and attended St. Louis School of Law; all of which he attributes to the continuous investment in him by his military supervisors, pastors, a life coach and numerous mentors. Knowing firsthand the importance of having a positive male role model, he committed to reaching back during his time in the USAF as a Big Brother, USAF mentor, and a sponsor for the Dept. of Corrections.

After serving abroad, John concluded his military service, working next for the Department of Defense, then as a Defense Contractor, and finally in the corporate sector. He continued mentoring young men as his calling to make a difference. As a father of 3 sons, John brings his parenting experiences together with his passion for writing and his heart for developing young men, into this inspired work that uncovers hidden issues facing Men who were Raised only by Women. John not only uncovers the issues, he provides candid and practical solutions, along with succinct mentoring goals, to help any mother, dad or mentor support and develop secure well-rounded young men.

Made in the USA
Charleston, SC
25 May 2015